CHERIE SCALF & KENNETH WATERS

DATING AND RELATING

A GUIDE FOR SINGLE CHRISTIANS

WORD BOOKS
PUBLISHER
WACO, TEXAS

DATING AND RELATING: A GUIDE FOR SINGLE CHRISTIANS

ISBN 0-8499-2890-7
Library of Congress Catalog Card Number: 81-71501
Printed in the United States of America

Scripture quotations in this publication are from the following sources:
  The Living Bible, Paraphrased (TLB), copyright © 1971 by Tyndale House Publishers, Wheaton, Illinois. Used by permission.
  The New American Standard Bible (NAS), © The Lockman Foundation 1960, 1962, 1963, 1968, 1971, 1973, 1975. Used by permission.
  The Amplified New Testament (ANT), copyright © 1958 by The Lockman Foundation.
  The New International Version of the Bible (NIV), published by the Zondervan Corporation, © copyright 1973 by New York Bible Society International.
  The New Testament in Modern English (Phillips), by J. B. Phillips, published by The Macmillan Company © 1958, 1960, 1972 by J. B. Phillips.
  The King James Version of the Bible (KJV).

The authors are grateful for permission to use copyrighted material that appears on the following pages:
  p. 5. From the song, "Lonely People," by Dan Peek and Catherine Peek, © 1974 WB MUSIC CORP. All Rights Reserved. Used by Permission.
  p. 36–37. From *Your Inner Child of the Past,* copyright © 1963 by W. Hugh Missildine. Reprinted by permission of SIMON & SCHUSTER, a division of Gulf & Western Corporation.
  p. 45–46. From the book, *The Hoax of Romance,* by Jo Loudin © 1981 by Prentice-Hall, Inc. Published by Prentice-Hall, Inc., Englewood Cliffs, New Jersey 07632.
  pp. 46, 120, 123, 124, 126. From *Sex for Christians* by Lewis B. Smedes, published by William B. Eerdmans Publishing Company. Used by permission.
  p. 98–99. From *Looking Out/Looking In: Interpersonal Communication,* First Edition by Ron Adler and Neil Towne. Copyright © 1975 by Rinehart Press, A division of Holt, Rinehart and Winston. Reprinted by permission of Holt, Rinehart and Winston.
  p. 127. From *The New Celibacy* by Gabrielle Brown. Copyright © 1980 by Gabrielle Brown. Used with the permission of McGraw-Hill Book Company.
  p. 129, 135–36, 141. From *Sex, Love, or Infatuation: How Can I Really Know?* by Ray E. Short, copyright 1978, Augsburg Publishing House. Used by permission.

First Printing, June 1982

Second Printing, April 1983

This is for all the lonely people,
Thinking that life has passed them by.
Don't give up until you
Drink from the silver cup.
You'll never know until you try.

—DAN PEEK AND
CATHERINE PEEK

Acknowledgments

CHERIE:

I wish to express my thanks to the men I've dated through the years. Each of you has contributed to the knowledge I've gained about male-female relationships.

My special thanks to my parents. Also, thanks to Margie and Joe Baumgartner, and Nancy and David Sterns, who opened their homes and their hearts to me during this writing project, and to Moriah Hood, whose professional counsel and loving support have greatly contributed to my emotional healing and personal growth, and thereby enhanced my writing contribution. And thank you, Kenny, for asking me to work on this book with you. You gave me the chance to try.

KENNY:

It would take reams to thank everyone who contributed in some way to my thinking and experiences. So I'll offer all of you a blanket "thanks." Special gratitude goes to the special women who laughed and cried with me as we grew together in a better understanding of God's plan for our lives: Diane, Marsha, Becky, Tina, Gayle, Marilyn, Sara, Cathy, Priscilla, Cherie, Mickie, and Diane. Those who have helped me survive the dateless nights also deserve mention: John and Kenna Smart; Britt and Carol Anderson; John and Gail Nall; Tim and Virginia Shepherd; my parents, Betty and Joe; and my grandparents, Bill and Edna Peterson. Finally, thanks to Julie Manning for providing helpful feedback as the book was taking form.

And a special thanks from both of us to Norma Stapenhill, who gave her wit and support—and typing skills—to this project and our marathon rewriting session.

Contents

DATING AND RELATING

The Conversation

In the beginning (over a quiet dinner at a Los Angeles restaurant) was the conversation ...

"Hey Cherie, I've had a thought for a couple weeks now and it won't go away. I think we should write a book on dating; you know, how single people relate to each other."

"Dating! Kenny, are you serious?"

"Sure."

"What'll we call it? *Fifty Ways to Lose Your Lover?* Or, how about *A Single Christian's Guide to Sadomasochism?* No, I know: *Broken Hearts, Shattered Dreams, and Boring Nerds!*"

"Hey, I'm serious. You've dated lots of men—some as friends, some romantically. Didn't you learn something? Wouldn't you ike to share it with others?"

"Well, yes, I have had some great experiences. But I'd rather forget some of the men I've dated."

"But even on boring dates I know you learned something. I've had some real snoozers. And blind dates ... forget it! I've sure had some embarrassing times, too. And of course I've been hurt. But I've also formed some lifelong relationships. Through snores and tears and all, I've learned some valuable lessons."

"I can relate to what you're saying, Kenny. I remember good times. And I've grown from the pain of rejection. I've learned much about myself and about men through dating."

"Now ya got it! Just think: do you know any singles who haven't dated? Do you know any that aren't concerned about relating to people of the opposite sex? I hear people asking all the time: 'Is she really the one?' 'Is he really the one?' 'What if she likes me more than I like her?' 'What if I like him and he doesn't like me?' Or the classic, 'Will I ever get married?'"

"We've talked about that last one before, Kenny. I really believe the Lord delights in blessing his people with marriage. It's all a matter of waiting for his perfect will to be revealed in his perfect time. No easy matter, I admit. And it seems to me that people who have the gift of remaining single all their lives usually know they have that gift. Don't you think?"

"Yeah, I agree."

"But if we're going to write a book about dating, I want to start with some real basic issues I've heard people discuss at singles' seminars. Things like where to meet people, how to ask them out, and how to enjoy a date. These are really important."

"I know. And Cherie, some friends of mine—especially those who are just divorced—feel really uneasy about dating. They say dating is like starting all over again in high school."

"A healthy self-image is so crucial. Lots of people suffer from shattered self-concepts after the death of a relationship. And of course, Kenny, we need to talk about sex."

"Gladly."

"Come on. I'm really bugged by sex games. I know it sounds like a stereotype, but men seem to feel they have to make a pass every time they go out on a date."

"It's just because you're irresistible."

"Be serious, Kenny. I have lots of friends who have been pressured to go to bed on the first date. They meet a man they really like and they are immediately asked to spend the night. When the woman says no, the man usually doesn't understand. The response is often, 'What's wrong with you?' Or, 'Don't you like me?' A woman can really feel pressured to go to bed with a guy just to keep dating him."

"Well, I know there's pressure. But women do some numbers on men, too. There are women who like to tease men, just to prove to themselves they are still attractive. Then, when the guy comes on, they get angry."

"Unfortunately, I know that's true."

"Also, men have this macho thing to contend with. It goes like this: 'If I don't make a pass, she'll think there's something wrong with me.' Some women think if you aren't aggressive you must not be all male."

"Seems to me men and women need to make some changes in the way they treat each other."

"Ain't that the truth. That could be the theme of our whole book."

"In addition to sex, I think we also need to talk about guilt. Lots of Christians who do go to bed with someone feel really guilty. They need to know God will forgive them if they make a mistake. We need to be true to Bible teachings and be practical, too. These are some really challenging issues to deal with."

"They sure are, especially since our society preaches sexual permissiveness. But I think it's only possible to have fulfilling dating relationships when we are living by Christ's principles. Anything else is second best."

"Right on."

(Silence.)

"Well, wanna give it a try? If we could answer half the questions we asked, it'd be a great book. I'd buy it."

(Silence.)

"Sure, Kenny, why not?"

... And so thus ended the conversation.

(With Kenny thinking, "What have I gotten into?")

(And Cherie thinking, "What a great idea—a book on dating!")

1.

Building a
Solid-Rock Foundation

So you want to date and relate, do you?

Great! That's what we're here to talk about. And we've got some exciting news. You can enjoy dating, and you can form deeply honest, caring relationships with members of the opposite sex. But these first few chapters won't be easy. We don't run a race to win without some preparation and conditioning. Athletes sweat and ache as they get into shape for their victorious race. It's going to take some "mental sweat"—honesty before the Lord—as you grow into a person capable of enjoying satisfying dating relationships. So in these first few chapters we will be building a foundation for future happiness.

The key to the enjoyment of relationships—and the enjoyment of life itself—is being "right" with God. All happiness flows from a strong relationship with our Creator. We believed this even before writing this book. But the Lord used a horrible event in Cherie's life to make it clear to us just how important this foundation is. We want to share with you the "mental and physical sweat" Cherie endured, as God showed her the value of a strong relationship with him.

Cherie's Comments:

I awakened early one morning and looked up at the bookcase clock. As I rolled over to go back to sleep, I saw a teenaged boy crouched on the floor between the nightstand and the bed. He leaped up and swiftly pressed his hand over my mouth. In startled confusion, I lay there a few seconds. My mind raced—"Is this a dream or reality?" Then my whole body convulsed in movement. I shook free of his hand. Immediately I said, "I rebuke you in the name of Jesus." He responded, "Now you are dead." Pulling a pipe from his pants, he hit me over the head. That crack seemed to echo to my toes.

An incredible struggle followed, much of which I can't remember, until he said, "If you'll let go of me, I'll let go of you." I
realized that we had rolled off the bed and he was sitting on top
of me and I was pulling his hair. I didn't let go. But he pulled
away. We continued to struggle with the pipe . . . I grabbed it
from him; he grabbed it from me, and then it flew out of our
hands. Quickly he grasped the drawer of the desk just above us
and pulled it open, frantically searching for something to use as
a weapon. He found nothing. So he choked me into uncon-
sciousness. In the last seconds, when I felt all life leaving my
body, peace wrapped around my heart. "Father, receive me into
your hands," I mentally whispered. Then all went inky black.

My screams brought me back to conscious awareness. I was at
the backyard gate, struggling to get out. "I'm alive, I'm alive!" I
kept thinking, "And now I'm going to lose my life because I can't
get this gate opened." I didn't know my hand was so battered
from trying to protect my head that it couldn't unlatch the gate. I
thought my assailant was still after me. I didn't know he had
left me for dead. I also had no recollection of getting off the
bedroom floor, or running through the house, or screaming in
the backyard. I just knew that I felt like a confused, trapped
animal as I continued to struggle with the gate, screaming. Finally the neighbors heard me and carried me to their home.
Quickly I was on my way to the hospital.

This attack happened while Kenny and I were in the process
of writing this book. For six months after the assault it appeared
that my injuries would prevent the book from ever being com-
pleted. It also appeared that my life would never be normal
again. My right hand was almost destroyed. My face had been
beaten into black and blue puffiness. Part of my scalp had been
torn off. For weeks the big accomplishment of my day was
brushing my teeth and taking a bath. I was so weak it took every
ounce of energy to drag myself to the bathroom to wash my face
and comb my hair. But that wasn't the worst of it. I was terrified
to close my eyes after dark. Night after night I tossed through
torturous hours, just waiting for the sun to rise so I could relax
and go to sleep.

In spite of these complications, I knew that I possessed the will
to return to normal. And during my recovery, people would occasionally comment that I seemed cheerful and confident. I can

only say that whatever cheerfulness I may have shown was the result of hours of prayer and study of the Bible. Somehow I didn't fall apart. Why? I have only one answer: the foundation of my life had already been established upon the strongest relationship I have ever known—my relationship with Jesus Christ. In that relationship I found hope for a complete recovery. And during that devastating time, God was my strength when no one else could help. He taught me the importance of having an intimate relationship with him as the foundation upon which all of life successfully rests. If I didn't have this foundation, I'm convinced I would not have recovered as I have.

We realize this story might seem a little melodramatic in the context of a book on dating. But it illustrates, better than any other way we know, just how important a strong relationship with God can be. We think it is important, also, to add that since Cherie's assault the Lord has continued to help her grow into a better awareness of who she is. Having survived that difficulty, she is now more open to him to teach her about how she relates to others. Some of those insights have greatly enhanced the ideas we will impart to you. You, also, have probably found that God brings growth to your lives through unpleasant events. And as you grow, the foundation-relationship with him is strengthened.

As we noted earlier, we were aware of the need for a strong foundation even before Cherie's tragedy. We needed only to look at the present-day state of male-female relationships. That, too, is a tragedy. It is no secret that our generation is experiencing a myriad of problems. The divorce rate is steadily rising. Some states in America report that almost one out of every two marriages ends in divorce. We look around us and view the dissolving marriages of relatives, friends—maybe even our own. At the same time, we see many other friends confused by dating games. We see some living in the frustration of bed-hopping—going from one partner to another, trying to find fulfillment in superficial relationships. It is apparent that changes need to be made in our attitudes and actions.

We believe the best time to initiate this change is not when a marriage begins to fall apart. It is at the beginning of relationships—casual dating and, later, romantic dating.

Courtship lays the foundation for a couple's future interaction
in marriage. Even when dating doesn't lead to a marriage
relationship, the times spent with another help us to better
understand ourselves and other people. We can learn valuable
lessons about how to relate to others through dating. And if we
learn the right types of attitudes while dating, we will have a
much more successful marriage.

That's why in the next few chapters we will discuss the importance of building a strong, Christ-centered self-confidence as
the foundation for successful dating. In this chapter we want to
talk about spiritual foundations. To do that we are going to go
all the way back to the creation of the human race. That is
when God created the first person—a man named Adam. This
one man laughed and cried and had intimate fellowship with
God. Before any other relationship existed, God established a
bond between a single person and himself. Then God said it was
not good that Adam should be without human companionship
(Gen. 2:18). So God made Eve. Immediately after God formed
her, there was a presentation to Adam—a marriage ceremony
of sorts. Adam is reported to have responded, "This is it! . . . She
is part of my bone and flesh! Her name is 'woman' because she
was taken out of a man" (Gen. 2:23,TLB).

God designed Eve to be a companion to Adam. She was different from her mate in appearance, mannerisms, and emotions, yet she was a helper and a friend suited to his needs
(Gen. 2:18). The author of Genesis goes on to say, "This explains why a man leaves his father and mother and is joined to
his wife in such a way that the two become one person" (Gen.
2:24, TLB).

When God made Eve, he had no intention of severing his
relationship with Adam. In fact, we are told that God now
included both Adam and Eve in his fellowship. Genesis 3:8
indicates that Adam and Eve knew "the voice of the Lord God
walking in the garden" (KJV); this infers that God had communicated with them previously. But it is in this same verse
that we are told Adam and Eve hid from God. Why? Because
they had done the one thing he had expressly forbidden. They
had eaten from the tree of knowledge of good and evil. For God
had told Adam: "Thou shalt not eat of it; for in the day that
thou eatest thereof thou shalt surely die" (Gen. 2:17, KJV).

What kind of death was this? A spiritual death—a separation from intimate fellowship with God. Adam and Eve had
been given the choice of obeying or disobeying God. When they
chose to disobey, they destroyed their perfect closeness with
their Creator.

And not only did their relationship with God suffer. Their
relationship with each other suffered. No longer having access
to the perfect source of wisdom and love, they began blaming
each other for their sin. In Genesis 3:12 we see that Adam tried
to blame Eve for the whole mess. Bert Hodges, writing in *His*
magazine, notes: "Adam set the pattern for broken marriages
for all time by trying to blame his wife for his eating. Even
husbands and wives find it difficult to be one flesh since the
Fall."[1] The Apostle Peter tells us in the New Testament that,
since Adam and Eve sinned, their seed—all future humans—
would also be corrupt (1 Pet. 1:23). So, even in the twentieth
century, we are inheritors of the failure-prone nature of our
first parents. The presence of this rebellious nature in us is the
reason dating is such a challenge—with occasional heartbreak,
misunderstanding, and the like.

Sounds dismal, doesn't it?

But take heed! There is a good side to this story!

It has always been God's plan to restore intimate fellowship
with his creation. The first part of that plan, as told in the Old
Testament, involved animal sacrifice as part of man's repentance for his sins. But this plan didn't offer intimacy with God,
because individuals kept on sinning and continually needed to
make animal sacrifices to atone for their sins. The means for
restoring intimate communion between God and man was
permanently established only when God chose to sacrifice his
Son, Jesus, as an offering to himself. This was a final, once-
and-for-all sacrifice. By allowing Jesus to be crucified, God
ended the need for continual sacrifices. A. Wetheral Johnson,
founder of the *Bible Study Fellowship* series, says, "Christ was
the *true fulfillment* of all which was symbolized by previous
burnt offerings when He represented fallen man . . . and offered
Himself as a 'burnt offering' to God in consecration and perfect
obedience *in our stead*."[2]

Then God raised Jesus from the dead. Jesus conquered
death. And he promised that anyone who believed in him

would not only have their sins forgiven by God, but would be given eternal life. Finally, Jesus said he would return unto his Father, but he promised to send a helper, the Holy Spirit, who would lead us into all truth and comfort (John 16:5-8).

This, then, is how God chose to restore what Adam and Eve had destroyed in the Garden of Eden when they broke fellowship with God. Now each of us has a choice: we can accept God's plan and the abundant life he offers, or we can stumble along in a confusion which will eventually end in eternal death. By taking the former option, being "born again," we enter into wholeness of mind, body, and spirit with God (Eph. 2:1-6).

Having been spiritually reborn, we are then able to establish an unshakable foundation, the type of foundation that enabled Cherie to withstand her ordeal. And it's this foundation that gives stability for every venture of life—including relationships. We can be like the wise man Jesus described in a parable—the man who built his house on a rock. When the winds and rains came, his house didn't fall, because it had a firm foundation (Matt. 7:24-27).

Faith in God offers us wholeness in all areas of our lives because we receive the Holy Spirit's help. When our lives are centered around this most important relationship, we form the basis for stability, strength, and wisdom in all other relationships. That is our central message in this book. When we "have it together" with Christ, we are much more likely to enjoy good dating relationships.

2.

Growing Closer To the Source

"Getting it together" with Christ is a lifelong process of being stretched and molded and blessed by the Holy Spirit. Jesus promises us that, if we want to have a strong foundation, we need only ask. In Luke 11:10 we are told: "Everyone who asks, receives; all who seek, find; and the door is opened to everyone who knocks" (TLB). A few verses later, Christ says that the Father will give the Holy Spirit to those who ask for him (verse 13). In Philippians 4:13 we read that we can do "all things" through Christ who supplies our strength. If you desire a foundation of strength in Christ, ask for it. God will supply it.

We must also, while asking, take personal responsibility for doing our part to grow closer to the Lord. Growth isn't just a supernatural, effortless process. Here are six suggestions for growing closer to God:

(1) *Establish a time of daily devotion*—no matter how difficult it might seem to squeeze in time between work, studies, or the children's needs. Take the time to read the Bible and pray. Pray for your day, for relations with the people you meet, and for the needs of others. Seek God's guidance, and you will be better able to live each day in fulfillment of God's plan for you. Ray Ortlund, in *Lord, Make My Life a Miracle,* says:

> There's one prime, basic, all-important place in your life where the rubber really meets the road.
> At this place, my friend, you win or lose—you make it or you don't.
> The place I'm talking about is where you go down on your knees, where you shut out all the rest of the world, and you and God, just the two of you get together.
> It has to be honest between you and Him.
> It has to be regular, at least once a day.

And it has to be fought for, clawed and scratched for—or it will never happen.

As sweet as life is to live with God moment by moment—and that's where it all begins—that doesn't rule out your need for a consistent encounter where it's just God and you.[1]

(2) *Keep a prayer list.* As prayer concerns come to mind, or are expressed by others during the day, keep a notebook handy and jot down the requests. Then, during your personal prayer time, bring these concerns before the Father. Keeping such a list allows you to keep track of answered prayers and to thank God for them. Having such a document of God's answers to prayers can be a great boost to our faith.

(3) *Submit yourself to a body of believers*—a church. Worship the Lord regularly with others. Become involved in social and spiritual activities of the body. We realize that, for some of you, finding a church home will take time. You may need to visit several congregations before you find one with the type of loving and accepting attitude you need. As singles, we often face a feeling of being outcasts in church. Some have been shunned, feared (especially by wives "protecting" their husbands from divorced women), and embarrassed (by insensitive matchmaking). To the discouraged single, Dr. Anthony Ash, editor of the "Single Again" newsletter, says,

> Remember two dynamic little words: *don't quit.* If brethren mistreat you, act as if you have become a second-class citizen, preach celibacy at you, constantly condemn you, etc., etc., just don't quit. Whatever inconsistency, lack of love, ignorance or lack of sensitivity others might manifest toward you; it is no ground for divorcing Jesus! So grip yourself. It won't be easy. Everybody won't be sympathetic, many won't care. Some will be outright mean and hostile. . . . But your prime concern isn't to judge their actions any more than it's their prerogative to judge you. Your purpose is to cleave to Him who promised He'd stick with you and trust you no matter what. Don't quit.[2]

(4) *Join a singles' group.* Church singles' groups, ideally, should provide fellowship with others, and you should also be able to share your concerns and needs in a prayerful atmosphere. Again, we know some of you might be reluctant to get

involved in singles' groups because of previous experiences. And we've occasionally heard the remark that singles' groups were for "losers." Don't believe it. Some fantastic relationships have been born in singles' groups, and some very discouraged people have been helped to wholeness through the ministry of their fellow singles. We encourage you to look upon a singles' group as a place to share yourself with others, to minister—this in addition to receiving ministry and meeting new friends.

(5) *Join a small-group Bible and prayer fellowship.* Most churches have group Bible studies that allow smaller networks within the body of the church to function as families. Meeting one night a week, you can share concerns and needs with a small group of supportive Christians.

Kenny's Comments:

To be truly effective, a small group must contain a core of committed Christians who go out of their way to serve each other. A small group should contain an atmosphere of openness. What is heard in the group should be considered confidential. Members should feel free to share problems and needs, both personal and theological. I have been part of the same small group for nearly two years. I look forward to Tuesday night because I know I will be enveloped in a cocoon of love. When I share needs, I know that seven other people will be praying all week for those needs. And I have the joy of upholding seven other people in my prayers all week. As a single person I have need of a close-knit family of friends. My small group provides that. Because of this love, I know I have grown closer to God.

(6) *Minimize temptations you face each day.* During a time of reflection, make a list of the influences on your life you don't think are positive. You might consider your television viewing habits . . . your selection of novels and magazines . . . your use of spare time. What are your friends like? Do they encourage you to grow closer to God? How do you spend your social time? Having written a list of influences that tempt you, ask God for help in avoiding temptation. Then make a conscious effort to sidestep the desire to do that which undermines the foundation you are trying to build in God.

Each of the suggestions we have explored in this chapter can help us build a strong foundation for dating by bringing us closer to God. They will not, however, make us exempt from loneliness, or from the comments of those around us who constantly remind us of that one simple fact: we are single. So coming to terms with that fact is an important part of building a solid foundation for dating relationships. In order to have a healthy dating life, we first have to learn that being single is OK.

3.

Single? It's OK!

Our attitudes about our singleness are extremely important. If we accept ourselves as single men and women, other people are more likely to accept us, too. Certainly you've met a person who exuded self-confidence, who by their smiles, their gestures, and their positive speech communicated a zest for life. And you were probably attracted to them. You wanted to get to know them better because their personality suggested they "had it together." In contrast, you may have met a person who was bitter about not being married. They made you feel uneasy; you didn't want to be in their company for very long because being with them was a downer.

In *The Challenge of Being Single,* Marie Edwards and Eleanor Hoover tell the story of a woman whose attempts to find companionship backfired. Elaine's story illustrates what can happen when we become desperate to establish a relationship:

> For the past three years since her divorce, Elaine, a librarian of thirty-four, had been returning each summer to a singles' resort in the mountains. She didn't particularly like the resort, but she had heard it was a great place for meeting men and she was increasingly desperate and intent on finding someone who could take her out of her single existence. The only trouble was things never seemed to work out romantically for Elaine. They would sometimes begin well but always fizzled disappointingly at the end.
>
> "Then [something] happened to set me straight," she says. "A man I was dating at the resort, whom I really liked, turned to me one night and said the most surprising thing. He said, 'Elaine, I don't think you really know how strong you come on with people—especially men. You've got the whole thing plotted there in your eyes—the desperate need to be wanted, the relationship, the marriage—the whole script. And you seem to want it so badly you could cry. I'm only telling you this because you're a nice,

interesting woman when you aren't caught up in the Big Romance game. You should cool it—you frighten men away.' I
didn't know what to say. I was so flabbergasted, but when I
thought about it later, I knew he was right."[1]

Elaine is not unusual. There are many singles who believe
that happiness will come only when they are in love. And they
live in a desperate search for that love. Neither of us wishes to
negate the fact that a unique happiness does exist in the love of
a man and a woman. But, at the same time, it is not romance
that creates long-lasting, deep personal happiness (We'll have
more to say on this later). Besides, as Marie Edwards says,
desperately seeking the "one-and-only" can be self-defeating:

> In any psychological or physical endeavor, we know that trying
> too hard usually generates so much tension that it makes reach-
> ing the goal even more difficult. If almost everything you do is
> motivated by the search of the one-and-only, you will inevitably
> miss out on most of the other values and benefits to be derived
> from your experience and from the people you have overlooked
> because they were not the sought-after one.
>   It is only when you stop or relax the search that you can allow
> another person to truly enter your life. Happiness, joy, delight in
> another—these are things that cannot be compulsively sought
> after. They are by-products of who you are, and how intelligently
> you have developed your mind, your heart, and your spirit.[2]

People who do not accept their singleness can also become
very bitter. They fall into the trap of blaming God for their
situation and blaming other people for not treating them right
in dating relationships. Instead of seeking to understand the
people they date, or searching for ways to offer their friendship
to those they'd like to date, they often see only their own needs.
Though crying inside for love and acceptance, they push other
people out of their lives by their desperate words and actions.

Kenny's Comments:
*Dale came to me a few years ago and said none of the women
in his graduate program would go out with him. He wanted me
to tell him why. It wasn't a chore I relished. I asked myself what
it was about him that I didn't like. I knew one thing I didn't like
was that he was always complaining about being lonely and*

never having anything to do. I mentioned that, and jokingly suggested that maybe he should get married. "I don't have time to get tangled up with some nagging lady," he snapped. Well, after that I figured I had a fairly good idea of the source of his problem. Then I asked a couple of women how they responded to Dale. They confirmed my fears.

"He's a real turn-off," they said. "He cuts everyone down and rarely has anything positive to say. It's obvious he's insecure about being single. He badly wants to be married. And he's become bitter because he isn't. That's why we avoid him. He's no fun."

I wish I could say this story has a happy ending, but it doesn't. I tried to delicately tell Dale that he needed to back off in his eagerness to find someone to date, to concentrate on accepting his singleness. That he should be just a friend to some of the women he knew. "I do accept my singleness," he huffed. Our relationship has never been the same. Even so, it is still better than his relationships with most women.

Dale's response may seem surprising. But many singles stubbornly maintain they have accepted their singleness, while inside they are confused and bitter. They continue to fantasize that "the right relationship" will suddenly appear. They fail to recognize that they are at least contributors to, if not the initiators of, their own unhappiness. John Fischer, author of *A Single Person's Identity,* made an interesting comment about people like Dale: "I have a strange feeling that a single person who is always wishing he were married will probably get married, discover all that is involved, and wish he were single again."[3]

Changing our attitudes and behavior is possible. We can do that through prayer, asking God to show us areas of our lives that need change. We can talk to friends who can lovingly provide feedback for us on qualities they see that might be altered. This process of inner growth takes time and patience. But God has promised that he will make us all he wants us to be. As he does, we will begin to exude more self-confidence and joy. And that, in turn, will attract more friendship and companionship.

We have a friend we'll call Sharon. She's in her mid-thirties and has never been married. She's attractive, but in a beauty contest she probably would not win many votes. That's relatively unimportant, however. Sharon has more than some women who hold impressive beauty titles. She glows. Her eyes and face light up a room. She exudes a happiness that says she likes people and life. Her actions prove she cares about others as she takes time to talk with them, and pray with them if necessary. So it's not surprising that she is rarely at a loss for male companionship.

"I wasn't always a happy person," she confided to us. "There was a time, when I was about twenty-five, when I was really mad at God. I was lonely and I didn't want to be single. I blamed him for making me remain only half a person—without a mate." Sharon said that one evening, while she was praying an angry prayer, the Lord began to show her that he wasn't to blame. Because he is perfect and loves her with perfect love, she realized, he wasn't the architect of her misery. She was causing her own loneliness through her anger and bitterness. Those traits made her the type of person no one—especially men—wanted to be around. So she asked God to help her shift her focus of concern from loneliness to godliness.

"I had to let go of the notion that happiness only occurs when you're with a special man," she said. "God showed me such thinking is a lie. He is the source of ultimate happiness. I still want to be married, when the right time and man come along. But most of all, I want to be a happy, fulfilled person—just as I am right now."

In addition to becoming more attractive to the opposite sex, like Sharon has become, there's another incentive for accepting our singleness. Such an attitude pleases God. It indicates that we have faith in his plan for our lives. We are told in Hebrews 11:6 that, "without faith it is impossible to please Him" (NAS). Grumbling and complaining indicates that we do not trust our heavenly Father to supply all our needs. But faith and trust produce hope for the future, and usher in a plan that is better than any we could devise.

God's Word on Singleness

As you know, two of the men who have had the most impact on world history were single: Jesus and the Apostle Paul. Both lived in a society that, like ours, stressed marriage. Jewish children were betrothed by their parents while still teenagers. To marry and produce children was consided a mark of success in the society. Singleness, in fact, is more accepted in our day than it was in theirs. Nevertheless, Paul exhorts people to remain single. "I wish everyone could get along without marrying, just as I do. But we are not all the same. God gives some the gift of a husband or wife, and others he gives the gift of being able to stay happily unmarried. So I say to those who aren't married, and to widows—better to stay unmarried if you can, just as I am" (1 Cor. 7:7-8, TLB).

This verse sometimes sends shudders down the spine of the single person longing for companionship. But let's look at it closely. First, we see that Paul is stating his preference. He is not giving a command from God. His preference may not be ours, and his words are not applicable to all of us. Second, we notice that Paul acknowledges marriage as the normal state. And he tells us that each of us has our own gift from God, either to remain unmarried, or to marry. Writing in *It's O.K. to be Single,* Mark W. Lee says: "Apparently one of the significant signs that one does not possess the gift to be single is the deep sense of sexual passion which might be interpreted as longing for a meaningful intimate relationship with a member of the opposite sex (1 Cor. 7:9)."[4] So from Paul's teachings we see that some have been gifted for singleness, some haven't.

Temporarily, however, all of us are single. While we wait for God's direction regarding our future state, what can we do now about our singleness? Paul suggests that we view it positively. In chapter 7 of 1 Corinthians, he tells us that "in the present time of stress it seems good to me for a person to continue as he is" (v. 26).

In verse 29, Paul goes on to say, "The important thing to remember is that our remaining time is very short, [and so are our opportunities for doing the Lord's work"] (TLB). How many of us view our singleness with the outlook that it enables us to give more time to the Lord's ministries?

"Paul is speaking very positively here," says John Fischer. "He elevates the state of singleness to the point where a person can give his undivided devotion to the Lord, can be totally set aside to please Him, with no conflicts of interest." Fischer cautions that Paul is not speaking against marriage, but stating a simple fact about discipleship and human nature. He continues,

> This truth has begun to set me free to realize that God has called me to live *now*. He hasn't called me to live four years from now. I don't know what is going to be happening four years from now. I have no idea. He wants me to realize my full potential... right now, to be thankful where I am, and to enjoy it to the fullest.[5]

Fischer's affirmation of his singleness is what God wants for each of us. Imagining situations or choosing to sacrifice what God has not asked of us is useless. When we are preoccupied with imagining the future—and thinking about a future mate—we miss God's call for obedience and service today. He asks us to accept our current state, being thankful for the opportunity to reach out and help others.

Do You Desire Marriage?

Do you want to be married? We believe most of you will be, in God's timing. If you are struggling with the fact that you are single and you don't want to be, we would like to encourage you. Share your concern and need with God. Trust him to begin a process of preparing you for your mate. Trust, we realize, is sometimes difficult when those lonely weekend nights and deep inner longings demand attention. The author of Hebrews encourages us with the statement, "Keep on patiently doing God's will if you want him to do for you all that he has promised" (Heb. 10: 36, TLB).

Ann Kiemel is a woman who exemplified this attitude towards singleness. Single until her mid-thirties, Ann struggled with the desire to be married. But she also used her singleness as an asset for helping others through an international ministry of writing and speaking. Several years ago she was interviewed by *Solo* magazine, and her comments illuminate what we feel is a realistic and healthy attitude towards singleness.[6]

Ann said she desired to be married and was looking forward to it. But she also said that she knows God wants her to use every minute—right now—to be a minister of his word. She acknowledged her struggle with loneliness, too. But when she felt lonely, she reached out to others—first in her neighborhood and later through her speaking engagements. She learned to accept her singleness, she said, when she became obedient to Christ. She then added:

> That didn't seem to be so important 5 or 10 years ago. But today I can see that obedience is the secret to fulfillment. If I had not tried to obey (and I have disobeyed many times), I would not be the woman I am today. And I still have a lot farther to go. But obedience has led me to this place of being centered.

The editors of *Solo* asked, "Obedience means no compromise, right?" Ann responded:

> People make so many compromises. And I think single people make as many or more compromises than anybody . . . especially in the area of sex—and in what they are going to pour their lives into—their mental perspective.
>
> Singles also compromise with their potential. They say, "I can't do as much, or be as creative. I'm not even expected to be quite as happy or productive because I'm single and I don't have the opportunities.
>
> Think of the possibilities! As a single woman I can bring children in and have them overnight or have couples over for dinner. And I'm very challenged by all the opportunities Jesus gives me in my neighborhood. For too many singles, it is just easier to compromise and not do their best.

Ann made another point we feel is important. That is, that *we* choose whether to be happy or unhappy in our lives. She put it this way:

> I have an option of being happy or unhappy. Some people think I was born a Pollyanna. Nobody is born a Pollyanna. You choose to be happy or unhappy. You choose to see the good in people or the negative in people. And I just think that most of life goes on in our minds and not in how we feel. And if we surrender that to God it can be very beautiful.

Wouldn't it be great if all of us could exude the type of trust in the Lord that Ann exemplifies? We can—if we are willing to continually seek God's will for our lives. Developing a positive attitude towards singleness will also require patience as God works to fulfill us. Coming to a complete understanding of who we are, and where God wants us to go, inevitably requires some soul-searching. In the process of this searching, most of us overlook one of the most important factors in determining the success of our relationships. Let's take a journey backwards and see what that factor is. . . .

4.

Beyond Childhood Expectations

There's another foundation to consider. It hasn't been built as well as the foundation God built for us in Jesus. That's because it is a human foundation. For some of us, it has been built very poorly; for others, it was built the best that was possible under the circumstances. That foundation, friends, is the one your parents or other significant adults built through their teaching and modeling in your lives. And, believe it or not, this influence is one of the most important factors determining the success of your relationships with others.

Some of you, especially those formerly married, know how differing expectations—often unspoken—can lead to some horrendous fights with your mate. Maybe you can relate to this situation sketched by a friend. In her family, the father helped with the dishes and cleaning the house. In her ex-husband's family, however, the mother performed those chores exclusively. Our friend said she expected help from her husband because that is what her father did. But her husband expected her to do all the work because that was the pattern in his household. Now, that wasn't the sole reason for our friend's divorce. But this example gives you an idea how certain unfulfilled expectations can lead to problems in relationships, often without our knowing what is happening.

In addition, unpleasant experiences of growing up may have resulted in repressed fears, anger, or hurt. As adults, we sometimes respond to circumstances in ways we can't even explain. Our behavior results from those childhood experiences that we've repressed. Psychologist Maggie Scarf, writing in *Psychology Today,* reports on a study of promiscuous behavior she conducted. She found that promiscuity often resulted from parental neglect in childhood:

This is true not only for men, but for women. The promiscuous female and the Don Juan are engaged in a similar—and similarly desperate—quest. Their search is for Caring Parent. And it is a search fueled by great fear and great rage. . . . [which results] from not having been cared for when one did so much *need* care and when one was so helpless and so vulnerable. Which is to say, when one was a child. The inner rage, then, is ultimately expressed by diminishing others: by using people for pleasure alone and thereby transforming them into Things, into Mere Objects.[1]

Hugh Missildine, author of *Your Inner Child of the Past,* takes this point about parental influences a step further. He says we are not only influenced by our parents; we also unconsciously internalize their teachings and actions towards us, so that we begin to treat ourselves as our parents did. And, in addition, we sometimes rebel against ourselves, just as we rebelled against our parents! This action by our "inner child of the past" sometimes crops up to trouble our adult relationships. Missildine tells the story of Linda:

Linda's life demonstrates how her "inner child of the past" kept her from doing what she wanted to do—marry and become a mother. An attractive but quiet girl with a self-contained air, Linda told me she was single and worked in a nursery school. She enjoyed working with children and they loved her. She wanted very much to get married and have children of her own. She had twice been engaged. But each time when the wedding date approached, she broke off the engagement in panic. . . .

Her mother had died when Linda was two. Then she lived with her grandmother who took care of her during the week. Her father kept her with him on weekends. When she was four, her grandmother died and her father hired a housekeeper. At six her father died. She then went to live with an elderly, rather formal, aunt and uncle who were childless. During her first two years in their house she had frequent nightmares but she was afraid to tell her aunt and uncle about them. She became a student and a "good girl" as she put it.

By the time she was grown, she had a vague but compelling feeling from her early experiences that to have a deep attachment to anyone was dangerous, the "kiss of death" for the person she liked. She kept all her relationships friendly, but distant.

This was the voice of her "child of the past." It had also spoken when, in spite of her wish to marry, the close relationship of marriage was near. If she allowed herself to feel deeply enough about someone to accept him as her husband he certainly would have been "taken away," as her mother, grandmother and father had been.[2]

You can see that Linda's fear of commitment is a result of her childhood experiences. But her story had a happy ending. Missildine goes on to say that Linda did eventually marry. Certainly many other problems besides a fear of commitment can be traced to childhood. Men may have difficulty showing tender emotions and affection because these emotions have been labeled "feminine traits," thus discouraged by parents. Both men and women may have difficulty with communication because no one listened to what they had to say when they were small—they quit expressing themselves and became ineffective communicators in adulthood. Many people struggle with shyness that developed because their parents didn't let them express themselves when they were small. Adults whose parents were overly critical of them as children can suffer from low self-esteem. And the list goes on and on.

Kenny's Comments:

For many years I wondered why I was attracted to fairly outgoing women—the type that usually were high school or college cheerleaders. I'm a more quiet and introspective person, and I couldn't figure out why I was attracted to women who, because of their personality, tended to dominate our discussions. But it felt comfortable. Then I confronted my own upbringing and found a clue. Both my mother and grandmother are outgoing. My father and grandfather are more reserved. The women in the family find it easy to meet people and engage in conversations. The men tend to have a more difficult time until they get to know someone well. Therein was the clue: my expectations for what an appealing woman was were based on what was familiar to me. Because the women in my family were outgoing, that was what I looked for when picking a woman to date. That's not necessarily a negative decision on my part. But because of the understanding I have now, I'm more open to dating quieter women. Some precious friendships have resulted.

Recognizing patterns from childhood that affect our behavior
today can help us relate better to others. Missildine provides a
list of nine parental behaviors that can cause negative behaviors on our part—because of our "inner child of the past".
We present this list in hopes you will find some "bits and
pieces" that might help you better understand some of your
feelings and behavior. (It is possible, we might add, to have
more than one of these "children" living inside you.):[3]

(1) *Perfectionism.* Perfectionists are often intelligent and
come from higher-income households. However, they feel they
were never really accepted by their parents, since they were
constantly encouraged and even pressured to "do better." As
adults, they put stiffer and stiffer demands upon themselves—
just as their parents did—to excel. The perfectionist likes to
control his or her environment. Failure is not handled well.
Perfectionists often demand perfection from those with whom
they associate, as well as from themselves.

(2) *Overcoercion.* A child who was overcoerced, always told
what to do by parents, often rebels with procrastination. That
was the only way of getting even with an overbearing parent.
People who were overcoerced often dawdle through chores and
do a half-hearted job. An adult who was overcoerced feels he or
she just can't get started doing things, and often feels too
exhausted to even try. They daydream excessively. Missildine
says this is the most common of "inner children."

(3) *Oversubmissiveness.* People who "got away with murder"
as children may grow up prone to temper outbursts and to
doing things on the spur of the moment. They might feel
unloved if people don't give in to their wishes. Oversubmissiveness, believe it or not, can coexist with overcoercion if one
parent was strong-willed and the other gave in too often.

(4) *Overindulgence.* People who are constantly bored and
unable to stick to certain tasks, always complaining,
seemingly unable to accomplish goals are probably being
dominated by an overindulged child of the past. Children who
have everything they want may feel bored, passive, and dis-
connected as adults. Whereas the oversubmissive syndrome
leads to impulsive behavior, the overindulged person tends to
be quite blasé about almost everything.

(5) *Hypochondriasis.* Hypochondriacs are overly concerned

about their physical health. Easily fatigued, they rarely participate in activities. Often hypochondriacs "acted" sick in childhood to get parental attention. That trait has carried over into adulthood.

(6) *Punitiveness.* A punitive person is trying to "get back" at his or her parents. Often he or she feels "bad" or "no good," and often punishes himself just as his parents did—perhaps by seeking work that requires him or her to take a lot of abuse. He or she is often cynical and bitter about life, carrying the proverbial "chip on the shoulder."

(7) *Neglect.* A difficulty in feeling accepted by people, a tendency to drift from casual relationship to casual relationship, and frequent feelings of loneliness are characteristics of people who were neglected as children. Neglect usually comes from being subjected to prolonged separation from one parent or the other. Missildine emphasizes that this type of neglect is not the type a child might feel if his or her father travels quite a bit. It is more prolonged and traumatic.

(8) *Rejection.* Those who don't feel accepted even by themselves, and who tend to be "lone wolves," might be suffering from rejection. Other signs are low spirits and low self-esteem. This might mean that as children they felt rejected by their parents or possibly abandoned because of a death or divorce in the family.

(9) *Sexual stimulation.* People who tend to emphasize physical aspects of relationships and are unrewarded in intimate relationships may not have had proper parental modeling about sexuality. Improper sexual attitudes can result from either of two extremes of upbringing: either a complete parental prohibition on the subject, resulting in fantasies, or overly seductive parental behavior which may instill a feeling that sex is an impersonal and purely physical activity.

This list of nine behaviors—and everything we've said so far—is provided to stimulate your thinking. It is by no means exhaustive, nor will it provide all you need for a proper psychological inventory. If you are really struggling with some aspect of your relationship with other people and we've caused you to do some deep thinking, we suggest you visit a professional counselor for further discussion.

Having catalogued these possible barriers to enjoying successful relationships, we want to stress that these barriers don't have to be permanent—it *is* possible to change! God desires to help us understand and then conquer any negative behaviors we have carried with us from the past. In her book, *Something More,* Catherine Marshall explains how we can begin to overcome our "inner children of the past." She calls this tendency to retain patterns learned in childhood the "law of the generations," and notes:

> Scripture continually insists on the principle of our connectedness as a fact of human life: We are . . . everyone members one of another. In this Law of the Generations, as I call it, we are linked to previous generations behind us. Our ancestors are in our genes, in our bones, in our marrow, in our psychological and emotional makeup. We, in turn, will be written into the children who come after us.[4]

Marshall traces some of her fears back to her paranoid grandmother. The grandmother would not even allow the house windows to be open at night because she feared germs would spread through the house. Marshall says she loathed her grandmother's fears, yet she herself developed an "overinclination to fear." She notes, "In my life it centered on a dread of germs and illnesses; a horror of mice or small dead animals, and during my childhood, fear of the dark, ghosts and the like."[5] Marshall goes on to say that she realized this fear was a sin, since she was acting out of a lack of trust in God. She encourages us that "He who is truth and therefore above the Law [of the generations] will do for us what we cannot do for ourselves. So there is not only hope, but a real answer."[6]

We can begin the healing process from our past by first admitting that we have carried certain weaknesses with us. Then, by praying about them and asking God for wisdom, we can discern how to change. During this time, we must open our hearts for enlightenment. Then the Holy Spirit can bring to our awareness the things that need to be corrected.

During this time of introspection, we suggest you begin focusing on past interactions that were frustrating or puzzling. Look inside yourself for some clues to how your upbringing and your "inner child of the past" may have contributed to the problem.

For example, think of a recent incident that was puzzling or painful to you. Recreate the scene in your mind. What did the people involved say to each other? What were you thinking? How did you react when the pressure was on? What expectations did you have that were not fulfilled?

As you visualize the scene, allow the Holy Spirit to reveal your shortcomings and the influences from the past that may have been working in that incident. Your mind may also wander to other similar incidents. Let it. That will help you form some idea about your patterns of behavior.

Working through all this will require much thinking and several phases of growth. In her Inner Healing seminars, Ruth Carter Stapleton has people focus on bringing Jesus into dark areas of their past, once these areas have been identified. "As we pray we are asking Jesus to come back into dark places and bring healing to the distressing and painful memories of the past," she says.[7] For instance, a person who may have felt rejection by a parent will relive a particularly distressing scene from his or her childhood, and then be instructed to invite Jesus into the situation. Instead of focusing on the memories of rejection, the person will be asked to visualize Jesus coming towards him or her with open arms. This visualization of the truth of God's eternal love helps heal the hurt of the past.

Catherine Marshall says that during this process of healing we must also forgive the ancestors who may have modeled or passed on such feelings. "First, having brought into the light all remembered dark heritage from previous generations, I had to forgive all these ancestors and release them from my judgment," she recalls.[8]

In this forgiving atmosphere, the healing love of God can change us. Marshall adds that, after she had forgiven her ancestors, she asked her son to pray for her. He prayed that she would be cut loose from her fears and that the Spirit of the Word would set her free. Her son then claimed a release for her in the name of Jesus. Marshall says that, after her son's prayer, she began praising God for every step of the process. "For we found that the release would not be final unless I received it in faith, and as I had been discovering, praise is the sweetest, surest route to faith," she added.[9]

So this is the process: identify the problem, pray for release and forgiveness, praise God for healing. The Lord, of course, might work in you somewhat differently. Some of you may be ready to make immediate changes; others may need more time to have the past revealed. Some may need professional counseling. We'd like to challenge you to be open—to be seekers. Don't blame others for past problems until you've looked inside yourself. Have you let the Lord build a good spiritual foundation? Have you identified your weaknesses that may have been caused by your well-meaning, but perhaps misguided, upbringing? If so, you will have a much better foundation for approaching relationships confidently.

Having said all this, we must add that there is one very dangerous line of thinking we have inherited from our parents and from much of society. And it has led us into a very grave sin—a sin that is as old as man.

5.

Can a Heart Divided
Find Real Love?

Cherie's Comments:
*Hesitantly, a friend read the verse: "The light of the body is
the eye: if therefore thine eye be single, thy whole body shall be
full of light" (Matt. 6:22, KJV). My friend said God had directed
her to share that verse with me. I was taken aback. I knew my
friend well enough to know that God had to be the one motivat-
ing her. But I couldn't understand what he was saying.*

*Having gone through a period of rebellion and indifference to
God, I had rededicated my life to him several years before. I had
made changes in my lifestyle. I had even said a hesitant "yes" to
his leading me into a ministry for singles. "What could be left?"
I wondered. "Was there still some hidden rebellion or stubbornness that was keeping me from growing spiritually?" I tried to
forget that troubling verse—but God didn't forget. And during
the next few months, he waited patiently until I was ready for
his teaching.*

*Meanwhile, my plans to find the right dating relationship
were failing. The harder I tried to make a romance work, the
worse things turned out. I despaired. I prayed more diligently
for understanding. In answer to my desperate prayer, God asked
a question: "Is the pursuit of romance the real God in your life?"
Immediately I denied it. I didn't pray to romance; I prayed to
God.*

*But the more I thought about that question, the more I
realized it could be legitimate. After another devastating
break-up, I cried out to God: "Show me anything you want. What
am I doing wrong? Why can't I find the right relationship?"*

*His answer cut deeply: "You want a human relationship more
than you want a relationship with me."*

No longer could I deny his words. I began to see that he wasn't

43

Lord of all in my life. If he was, I would trust him with my dating relationships. And I wouldn't fall apart when one ended. Although God had a place in my heart, in reality his crown rested above an empty throne. I was looking for someone human to take his seat. I worshiped God and I was very involved in Christian service. Yet in my heart I was so busy pursuing human love and affection that I had put God in second place. Such a subtle sin!

My desire, I had felt, was normal. I didn't think my desires for romance were different from those of many people I knew. But God had broken through my stubborn resolve to show me that I had put my heart's desire of romance before my relationship with him.

I'm thankful he brought this problem to my attention so I could begin to deal with it. Hebrews 4:13 tells us, "And there is no creature hidden from His sight, but all things are open and laid bare to the eyes of Him with whom we have to do" (NAS). I had been blinded to what was really happening in my life, but God was not.

Does Cherie's story sound familiar? We bet it does. A worship of romance is one of the most subtle and widespread attitudes that destroys relationships—before they even get a chance to form. The worship of romance, in fact, any attitude or action that hinders our relationship with Christ, minimizes the possibility that we will enjoy fulfilling dating relationships.

Another name for attitudes or actions such as these is *idolatry.* In Exodus 20:3, God told the Jews: "You may worship no other god than me" (TLB). In Leviticus 26:1, God says: "You must have no idols; you must never worship carved images, obelisks, or shaped stones, for I am the Lord your God" (TLB). Much of the Old Testament is a chronicle of God's wars against the idols the Jewish people erected. The Jews turned their backs on God and worshiped the Golden Calf just after receiving the Law from Moses in the Sinai Desert. So God made them wander aimlessly for forty more years. Charles H. Spurgeon, noted for his thoughtful Biblical commentary, says:

The whole history of the human race is a record of the wars of the Lord against idolatry. It was divine jealousy which moved the

Lord to bring all His plagues on Egypt. Careful reading will show that those wonders were all aimed at the gods of Egypt. The people were tormented by the very things they had made to be their deities.[1]

The authors of the Amplified Version of the Bible explain idolatry as "false gods, . . . anything and everything that would occupy the place in your heart due to God, from any sort of substitute for Him that would take first place in your life]" (1 John 5:21). A contemporary list of idolatrous sins includes immorality, greed, slander, drunkenness, thievery, adultery, homosexuality, and lying (1 Cor. 5:11, 6:9; Rev. 21:8). To that list we add the obsession with romance and a few other idols we will discuss in a moment.

The Deception of Romance

Evidence that romance sometimes replaces God comes from a thoughtful book by Dr. Jo Ludin, *The Hoax of Romance*. Dr. Ludin chronicles the rise of the romantic ideal in our culture, an ideal she says has created "stifling dead-end relationships by building impossible dreams in our own minds, fantasies totally unrelated to the reality of our feelings for each other and the business of living together under the same roof on a day-to-day basis."[2] She blames many of the problems of contemporary relationships on this antiquated idea of romance, an ideal which was formalized—believe it or not—in the twelfth century with a queen named Eleanor of Aquitaine.

Eleanor, who was married to Louis VII of France and later Henry II of England, set up a school in France to teach the finer things in life to wealthy young women and their would-be male suitors. Eleanor and her daughter, Countess Marie of Champagne, refined a code in which the suitors vied for the affections of the ladies through poems, songs, and other acts of courtship. They encouraged the enticement of jealousy as a test of whether a man was truly in love; they fostered the ideal that a flashy suitor would swoop a woman right off her feet, making her insane with love. These women, and also Andreas Capellanus, who wrote *The Art of Courtly Love*, drew heavily upon the writings of Greek poet Ovid, and the mythology of King

Arthur's "Camelot." While some of their teachings are little more than common sense and courtesy, other teachings are potentially more damaging. Some examples are:

—Every lover regularly turns pale in the presence of his beloved. When a lover suddenly catches sight of his beloved his heart palpitates. A man in love is always apprehensive.

—He who is not jealous cannot love. Real jealousy always increases the feeling of love.

—He who wants to make a real test of the faith and affection of his beloved should, with the greatest care and subtlety, pretend to her that he desires the embraces of some other woman....

—If love diminishes, it quickly fails and rarely revives. Love can deny nothing to love.

—[A woman] must be careful not to let him know her real intentions, and she must hide her real feelings.[3]

Well, you get the picture. We aren't saying that all of these ideals are still with us, but in more subtle forms we are still captive to a system based on "love traps"—dishonest communication and romantic games. Slavery to this romantic ideal can ruin relationships, because it creates unfulfillable expectations between the man and the woman. Lewis B. Smedes, writing in *Sex for Christians,* says, "It is simple to make an idol: slice one piece of created reality off the whole and expect miracles from it."[4]

No matter what your expectations are, women, there are no knights in shining armor to steal away your heart. And men, there are no perfect fair damsels in distress. Enticement to jealousy, emphasis on emotional love, and romantic gameplaying are not ways to have an open, honest relationship. As Dr. Ludin notes, all of this stress on superficialities leads to the installment of Romance as an idol:

By making love the force that can create or enhance the Good in man, [this way of thinking] substitutes love, and its agent, woman, for God. No longer does man have to seek the Good, or

God. . . . All he has to do is wait for love to strike and for love's signs to be revealed for him (or her) through the emotions. He doesn't have to think about it, only wait passively for love to arrive. Once it grips him the lover is compelled to follow love's dictates. He cannot escape, so he might as well submit to love's power, stronger by far than his own.[5]

Kenny's Comments:
There have been periods in my life when I have really struggled with this idea of elevating romance. Most of us have grown up in an age where everything from toothpaste to cigarettes is trumpeted as a love potion. If we use the right toothpaste, we will find romance. If we smoke the right cigarettes, we'll be macho and women will love us. Implicit in this devious advertising, and the other cultural trappings that go with it, is the idea that, if we aren't coupled, we aren't complete people. Pretty soon the constant barrage of this trash sinks into our subconscious minds. We begin to have the same expectations of romance that our society has.

I realized this, like Cherie did, when my relationships began failing. I retreated to a dream world—it was much easier that way. Every time I would meet someone new, I'd hardly give her a chance to become a friend. If she didn't measure up to my dreams, I turned her off. And when I did meet someone who measured up, I came on so strong she ran from me. It was only when the Lord allowed me to go through a long string of failures and loneliness that I began to listen to his message. He comes first; my desires for romance and companionship come second. That's the route to true fulfillment.

Seven Subtle Idols

We hope you'll be less stubborn than we were and that our list of seven idols will provide a helpful checklist. We hope you'll evaluate your attitudes and behavior against it. If you find you are "worshiping" any of these things, then by all means submit your problem to God and ask for his power to help you in smashing them:

(1) *Incessant dreaming.* Fantasizing can become idolatry if we let our minds dwell so much on the dream that we begin to

have troubles living in reality. We might drift through a whole day in a dream world, picturing various scenes in our minds. Maybe you're on a windswept coast, nestled together under the protection of a tree . . . and he kisses you. Or she slips a note under the windshield of your car that says, "All is forgiven. I love you." Daydreams. They are enjoyable, and a good creative release, but when we elevate them to the point that we avoid relationships with real people, we miss something special. And if our daydreams become our standard for relationships, we will be sorely disappointed.

(2) *Worship of past relationships.* This can be a particular problem for the formerly married who may not have completely accepted the end of their past relationships. But whether we were married or not, if we constantly look back and hope instead of looking forward to new challenges, we idealize our past relationships to the point that bad events from the past don't seem so traumatic—only good memories remain.

Then we may begin to judge every new person we meet by the "him" or "her" of the past—now highly idealized. Of course few people meet those standards.

Some indications that you might be worshiping a past relationship are:

—You jump every time the phone rings, because you still hope it is he (she) calling.
—You're obsessed with guilt over what you said the last time you saw her (him).
—You fantasize that he (she) is at the door, with tearstained cheeks and bended knee, begging you to take him (her) back.
—You still devise ways to entice your love to come back into your life.
—You pump your children or friends for information about what your "ex" is doing, who she (he) is dating, and whether or not you are missed.

To truly be healed of this hurt, you must be willing to let go of that past relationship. Put it behind you and look forward. Ask God to heal hurts and help you develop more realistic expectations. Then be open-minded about new friends. More than one couple we know have said that they really weren't romantically attracted to each other at first. But as they got to know each other as friends, and overcame initial reservations, a love grew. They eventually married. What would have happened if they had been worshiping past relationships and refused the opportunity to get to know each other?

(3) *Immorality.* Fornication (sexual impurity) and adultery are linked with idolatry (1 Cor. 10: 7,8). Enjoying sexual intercourse outside marriage is placing our desire for physical satisfaction above the desires of God to make us complete and whole in every area of our lives. Placing our physical needs first can impede God's blessings in our lives. Placing his plan for us first insures that all our needs are met.

(4) *Covetousness.* Ephesians 5:5 tells us that a covetous person is also an idolater. Envying someone else's dating opportunities constitutes idolatry. So can jealousy of the happiness of a friend. If we "wish enviously" for a relationship enjoyed by a friend, we are committing idolatry.

(5) *Stubbornness.* 1 Samuel 15:23 says, "Stubbornness is as bad as worshiping idols" (TLB). How do you respond when God speaks to you about something you may not want to do? Are you obedient? Or do you defend your actions? Maybe you ignore the Lord altogether. Listen to his voice of direction, so that you may really enjoy the abundant life he wants to give.

(6) *Vanity.* In Ecclesiates we hear, "Vanity of vanities . . . all is vanity" (12:8, RSV). How much time and money do you devote to making yourself look attractive to the opposite sex? In Jeremiah 2 we are told that God confronted excessiveness by telling his people: "How you plot and scheme to win your lovers" (v. 33, TLB). God reminded them that they had turned their backs on him in their rush to win friends. Our physical appearance *is* important—as we'll discuss later. But if we have an obsessive desire to look just right in order to attract others, we are committing idolatry.

(7) *Frantic searching.* In Jeremiah 2:23, idolatrous Israel is likened to a camel running hither and thither in search of a mate. God asked the Israelites, "Why do you go around so much changing your way?" (v. 36, NAS). Are you like the Israelites? Do you change circles of friends or churches in search of someone to date? Is your social life characterized by a

series of unfulfilling, short-term relationships? If so, you may
be more intent on seeking dates or companionship than you are
on seeking after God. As a consequence, your relationship with
him—and your relationships with others—will suffer.

As you may have noted already, many of these points present
a problem only when they are out of balance in our lives. When
we are obsessed with anything, we fall short of God's plan for
us. And the more we lean toward the *things* we want, the more
imbalanced we become. But no matter how attractive and exciting these things may appear, they will fizzle in the end. And
while they are fizzling, our loving God may find it necessary to
discipline us: "For the Lord corrects and disciplines every one
whom He loves, and He punishes, even scourges, every son
whom He accepts and welcomes into His Heart *and* cherishes"
(Hebrews 12:6, ANT). We can be thankful for his corrections.
"Should we not ... cheerfully submit to God's training so that
we can begin really to live?" asks the author of Hebrews (12:9,
TLB).

If you are experiencing frustrations in your dating relationships, look within to see if you are "out of balance." Ask God to
show you if you are harboring any idols in your heart. He can
reveal the truth, and help you overcome any idolatrous desire.
Ask for a new measure of faith, and trust that he will order
your friendships with members of the opposite sex.

Many of us are sitting in a dark little room of life, bound, and
looking to our idols, such as Romance, for help. All the while,
Jesus is standing at the door, waiting for us to let go of these
things so he can give us something better. He wants us to have
an abundant life (John 10:10) with all the friendships we can
handle. So smash your idols. And let him guide you to some
truly exciting friendships.

Then, go look in the mirror. Do you like what you see? Well,
if not, let's do something about it. First impressions *are* important, you know.

6.

Making First
Impressions Count

Suppose you're at a party and a friend says she wants to introduce you to John. John is an accountant with a great personality, you are told. Furthermore, he owns a few apartment houses and drives a Porsche. He worships at a church in your denomination. Sound too good to be true?

Then you meet him. John is six-foot-one with a dark complexion. His hair is uncombed and curling around his ears. There are white flakes on his red and green plaid polyester blazer. His open-collar shirt isn't ironed. He's wearing light brown pants and unpolished black wingtips. And he's thirty pounds overweight.

So much for that great idea!

A few minutes later, your friend says she wants you to meet Dave. She explains that he's an insurance salesman, about your age, with a master's degree in business. He just moved to town and has joined your church.

This time you wonder if you should get your hopes up. But you decide to meet Dave. Nothing ventured, nothing gained, you reason. Dave is wearing a light brown pullover sweater, with the collar of his white shirt showing. He's wearing tan wool pants and polished brown oxfords. His hair is combed, and his moustache is neatly trimmed. His facial features are pleasant, but not strikingly so. And his build is just average.

You've just met two men of equal abilities, age, wealth, and religious leanings. Which one was most attractive to you?

Why, Dave of course.

Why?

Well, he's better dressed and he seems to care more about himself by the way he looks.

Let's go one step further. How would you answer these questions:

—Which man seemed more dependable?
—Which man seemed more sensitive?
—Which man seemed more "together"?
—Which one would you like to get to know better?

Again, we bet you picked Dave. Does this little exercise give you some clues as to just how important first impressions can be? We often make judgments about whether we want to be friends with someone on the basis of initial impressions. And we often make decisions about character strictly from the way a person looks. As time goes on, we might get to know a person for who they really are. Even in our example, we might eventually find John to be a much more sensitive and spiritually sound person. But most of us would not even take the time to get to know John, simply because the way he looked caused us to make some judgments about his character and attractiveness. That's unfortunate, but it is the way most of us have been taught, and that teaching runs deep within us.

In a world teeming with messages about sexual standards that stress physical beauty, we are continually made aware that in physical terms we fall short of a perfect "10." For the Christian, however, the most important aspects of attractiveness don't lie in physical appearance. So we don't want this chapter to invoke any feelings of inadequacy. But we do want to encourage you to look your best—to show you care about yourself by doing all you can to "put your best foot forward."

The way we look influences the way we feel. Psychologists who study nonverbal communication tell us that when we look our best we tend to be more confident about ourselves. Physical-education specialists Dave Coffman and Lee Nicoloff note that good conditioning "improves one's physical health, physical appearance and body image with concomitant increase in self acceptance."[1]

Probably the most important reason for doing what we can to improve physical appearance is that it pleases the Lord. Paul tells us that our bodies are temples of the Holy Spirit (1 Cor. 3:16). God actually lives inside us! What kind of temple do you think he wants to inhabit? A temple with peeling paint and broken windows? Or a modest chapel with cleanly trimmed lawns and freshly painted walls? Take pride in the fact that the Creator of the universe is living inside you. Do what you can to reflect his presence in the way you look. When you do, you will greatly increase your chances of making strong and favorable first impressions on the people you meet.

Here are a few suggestions to help you:

(1) *Dress modestly, yet fashionably.* Fashion designer Halston says, "Don't let clothes wear you. You must learn to relate fashion to yourself in the simplest, most comfortable, most attractive terms. Don't let fashion frazzle you. It should be easy. Easy and comfortable. The key is 'simple is best; less becomes more.'"[2] Gini Andrews, author of *Your Half of the Apple,* reminds us that an extreme of dress—either flashy or drab—calls attention to us and says something about us. "People stare and notice and point and yes, I'm talking about dull clothes as well as the opposite extreme."[3] And Diane Blacker, author of *Harmony,* notes that as Christians it is our responsibility to dress with neat, well-coordinated clothing that does not detract from the beauty of Christ that is in us.[4]

Men, refer to magazines like *Gentlemen's Quarterly,* or books like John Molloy's *Dress for Success* or Egon von Furstenberg's *The Power Look* (available at your local bookstore). Use these as educational tools, as starting points. Both provide information about various styles and "looks" to suit different personalities and budgets. You might also walk through a shopping center and see what is currently being sold as fashion. Be sure to go into both "young look" stores and more conservative stores catering to businessmen. Having done some research into the spectrum of styles, decide which best suits your body build and personality. Then make some judicious purchases. You might also get some advice from a female friend who can give an opinion on styles and colors.

Women, basic information on dress is available from magazines or a stroll through clothing stores. John Molloy has also written the *Woman's Dress for Success Book,* catering mainly to professional women who want to advance at their jobs. Diane Blacker's *Harmony* is another good book on putting together a wardrobe. Ms. Blacker advises that women choose garments that can be mixed and matched. "Two or three outfits can be switched around to make six," she notes.[5] If you are in doubt about styles or colors, ask a friend. Or take a class in fashion coordinating from a local community college. You'll learn how to choose colors and styles, in addition to receiving tips on make-up and other beauty secrets.

One word of caution about clothing for both men and women. Fads come and go, but basic, high-quality clothing styles change only slightly. Don't build your entire wardrobe around the latest craze. Rather, choose fashions that are basically conservative in nature and will last through several years of fashion changes.

(2) *Good grooming is essential for a good appearance.* "The first thing I notice about a man are good manners, neatness and cleanliness, in that order," notes Diane Blacker.[6] Neatness and cleanliness fall under the category of good grooming.

Kenny's Comments:

Good grooming to me means that a woman looks clean. By clean, of course, I mean her hair is combed, and her make-up is appropriate to the size and shape of her face—not caked on. Cleanliness says healthiness, and I feel that is what most men desire when they date a woman.

(3) *Watch what you eat.* Donna Axum tells us:

Food not only determines your shape, it also affects the health and beauty of skin, nails, teeth, hair and eyes. Dark circles under your eyes, sallow complexion, limp, dark hair; clogged pores, frown lines—all are a reflection of our poor health habits. An intelligent and informed approach to eating lays the ground work for health and beauty. It must become a way of life.[7]

There are many books on proper nutrition in the marketplace. Most tell us to eat a balanced diet with the proper blend of proteins, carbohydrates and unsaturated fats. We should avoid refined sugars, caffeine, saturated fats, overly processed grains, and too much salt, because these substances negatively affect blood sugar balance and cholesterol levels in the body. Drowsiness, lack of energy, and depression can result from poor nutrition. Poor diet can also contribute to problems in relationships. In fact, Dr. Maryjane Hungerford, a marriage and family counselor, claims that many of the marriage problems she has studied can be linked in part to poor nutrition.[8]

Speaking of eating, if you need to diet, do so. But first have a thorough medical examination and seek professional guidance for your weight reduction program. Fad diets usually don't produce lasting results, and they can endanger your health. Eating a variety of foods is important for maintaining a proper intake of vitamins and minerals. And, if you need them, take vitamin and mineral supplements.

(4) *A healthy body requires exercise.* The heart needs stimulation for blood circulation. The muscles need to be toned and stretched. Most of us associate exercise with jogging. But there is a variety of enjoyable ways to exercise—including aerobic dancing, racquetball, basketball, dancing, and swimming. A helpful book on exercise is *Aerobics* by Dr. Kenneth Cooper, (available at local book stores). It explains in detail the types of exercises that will help you look and feel better. Many other books on exercise are now on the market. Choose carefully; there is no "get healthy quick" approach. Exercise must be vigorous enough to stimulate the heart and induce perspiration. And it must be regular—at least three times a week.

A few hints about exercise: exercise at the same time of day if possible; start slowly and build up gradually; don't try to do too much at once or you will hurt yourself. If possible, pamper yourself after exercise with a jacuzzi or sauna bath. If not, take a long bath in the tub at home.

Stretch before and after exercising. This increases the flow of oxygen and other nutrients to the muscles and aids in the prevention of muscle pulls and tears.

And choose a friend to exercise with, whenever possible. It's always easier when two of you have each other for motivation and encouragement.

Proper dress, diet, nutrition, and exercise all play an important part in improving physical appearance. For the sake of making good first impressions and meeting new people, you should make sure you are doing all you can to look and feel your best. Of course, no matter how good you look and feel, you won't make much headway in dating if you are sitting home. You've got to get out and meet people! And that is easier than you might think!

7.

The How and Where of Meeting New Friends

To put into practice all we've said so far, you need to "get into circulation" and meet new friends. There are more ways to do it than you think. But first, you have to get to work. Dr. Joyce Brothers provides us with some sensible counsel about meeting new people:

> Be visible. The man who spends his spare time watching television, the woman who rarely leaves the house, the office workers who hold themselves aloof and scurry home to lonely evenings, people who do not involve themselves with others seldom find love (and research also shows us that they die at a younger age than those men and women who are more extroverted). One rarely trips over a prospective wife or husband between the television set and the refrigerator. You have to let the world know that you exist and show people that you are interested in them. Finding love is like catching a fish; you have to have your lines out.[1]

Dr. Brothers is right. We need to get out and meet new people. There may be an occasional rejection, but don't be discouraged. Try again.

We've prepared a list of eleven ways to meet new people. The list is by no means exhaustive. We hope it will help you think of some other creative ways and places you might make new friends.[2]

(1) *At church.* Have you met everyone at your church? Make sure you are friendly and open to meeting new people. If you are part of a very large church, make a point of trying to meet at least one new person each week.

(2) *Join a club or organization of interest to you.* These may range from Parents Without Partners to the Sierra Club. Many

organizations are listed in local newspapers. Also, there is a national reference book of organizations, the *Encyclopaedia of Associations,* available from Gale Press in New York City. Your local library should have a copy.

(3) *Do volunteer work for the political party of your choice.* You'll meet people of similar political beliefs, and as a volunteer you can render many services to a party or candidate. One of the more interesting kinds of campaigning is to host a "coffee klatsch." These gatherings enable local candidates to meet voters face-to-face in small numbers and comfortable settings. And they can enable you to meet your neighbors and people whose views are similar to yours. The klatsches usually cost you little or nothing, because the campaign organization will help with the invitations and refreshments. All you need to do is volunteer your house or apartment.

(4) *Take an evening class at a local high school or college.* Adult education is quite popular today; people of all ages— many single—are having fun and learning at the same time. Or maybe you'll want to go back to school and earn a college degree. Impossible? Not so. Most schools now offer evening courses, so it's possible to attend school and still work. A few years ago we met Denise, a student at Los Angeles City College. She was 62 and working towards a public relations degree. "I couldn't sit around feeling sorry for myself after my husband died," she said, "so I went back to school. I keep young by talking with the college-aged students. Also, I've met some people my own age and we occasionally go out for dinner together. I'm learning and making new friends at the same time."

A special note to women: several groups make scholarships available to women who want to begin or continue their education. One program, the Career Advancement Scholarships, gives help to women who are at least twenty-five and whose studies have been interrupted—and this includes women who plan to return to school part time. The scholarships pay full or partial tuition, books, child care and transportation. Second Career Scholarships are for women who are at least thirty and who have become displaced homemakers through the death of a spouse or the dissolution of a marriage. (For futher information, write the Business and Professional Women's Foundation, 2012 Massachusetts Avenue N. W., Washington, D.C. 20036.)

(5) *Learn a new sport or hobby.* Active involvement in a hobby or sport brings many rewards. Besides increasing your chances of meeting potential dates, you'll enjoy yourself at the same time. You can choose from photography; arts and crafts; games such as backgammon, chess, or bridge; cooking; music; snorkling or Scuba diving; or amateur drama. Sports may pay even greater dividends if you are concerned about bettering your health. We've already mentioned some good exercises. The key is to find people at work or in your apartment complex who are interested in "working out" with you. You might put a note on the bulletin board asking for jogging or hiking partners. You might get some interesting responses.

(6) *Change jobs.* If you are bored or feeling unfulfilled in what you are doing, search for a more rewarding job. Feeling socially isolated several years ago, Kenny decided to seek a position in an organization with more Christians. He was eventually hired by World Vision, where he has had the opportunity to meet a number of Christian women his own age. "It's never too late to switch jobs, even if you need to reeducate yourself," a friend told us recently. At age twenty-nine, she is enrolled in a graphic arts program at a local college, and plans to switch jobs once her studies are complete.

One word of caution, though. Switching jobs in search of romance is as impractical as changing churches in search of new friends. We suggest you consider switching jobs only if you are actually dissatisfied with the work. The need to have a more exciting social life can be a consideration, but we don't feel it should be the only motivation.

(7) *Get involved in groups supporting important social issues.* These might be local campaigns, such as one against pornography, or national issues like nuclear energy legislation or bills affecting religious freedom.

(8) *Senior singles may meet others through community senior citizens' groups.* YMCAs and YWCAs host activities for seniors, and seniors may also volunteer for two service groups sponsored by the U.S. government. SCORE is an acronym for Senior Corps of Retired Persons, an organization through which former business people volunteer to assist small busi-

nesses. Your local SCORE office can be reached through the U.S. Small Business Administration office in your area.

Another program of note is Foster Grandparents. Foster Grandparents volunteer several days a week (receiving a small stipend) to act as "grandparents" to physically and emotionally disabled children. The nearest Foster Grandparents' office can be reached by calling the ACTION office of the federal government.

Obviously, if you are a senior who chooses to volunteer through such an agency, you won't meet many people your own age while actually discharging your duties. But you'll meet a few, and through seminars and parties hosted for volunteers you'll have opportunities to meet many more people.

(9) An option for those seriously seeking marriage is the *Scientific Marriage Foundation.* SMF is an interdenominational bureau dedicated to introducing marriage-minded people. In its thirty years of operation, SMF has matched more than ten thousand couples, with a divorce rate of only 1 percent. Individual applications are screened by qualified counselors (usually local pastors), and all efforts are made to introduce people who are similar in ten areas: age, marital history, height, geographic location, religion, education, habits, occupation, race, and personality traits. (More information on SMF can be obtained by writing The Complement Club, Hopkins Building, Mellott, IN 47958.)

(10) *Organize a party circle.* A party circle is a group of people who pool contacts for parties. The parties are held in the homes of the members on a rotating basis, and everyone shares the cost. The idea is for each member to invite a new person of the opposite sex for each party, thereby extending his or her contacts. And you don't need to eliminate someone because you are not romantically attracted. One of your friends might really fall for him or her!

Other party ideas include: Christmas season open house; a party for a friend who just got a new job, a promotion, started a business, or had a birthday; a potluck buffet; a series of round-robin birthday parties (form a committee with two friends and alternate throwing birthday parties for each other); and Sunday brunches.

(11) *Vacations.* Consider taking a singles' vacation. Some are

for swingers, so plan carefully. There are many tours, though, through larger singles' groups at churches, or through Christian travel agents. These are excellent opportunities to meet new people.

You might also try "work-your-way" weekends. Some resorts will let you trade a skill (secretary, clerk, nurse, doctor, typist, waitress or waiter, bookkeeper, reservations clerk, etc.) for your weekend's lodging. There are many smaller resorts that welcome this type of help.

We hope these eleven ideas have been helpful. As you've read this list, you may have noted that two popular places to meet people—singles' bars and dating bureaus—have been omitted. There's a reason for this. Singles' bars are the place most people go to pick up or be picked up. This is one of the reasons they are often referred to as "meet markets." Many singles in bars are lonely—so lonely they will consent to a night of sex with a stranger just to avoid going home alone. This instant pairing for sexual gratification—or a disappointing, unproductive evening which makes us feel "cheapened"— is often the outcome of a night at a singles' bar. Such places are counterproductive to the goal of establishing caring, supportive relationships. The chances of meeting someone with similar goals, religious beliefs, and other important qualities are extremely slim.

To counter the singles' bar phenomenon, some Christian groups have started coffee houses and Christian "nightclubs." These are welcome alternatives to the blatantly sexual appeal of singles' bars. Unfortunately, most Christian entertainment establishments are short-lived. The best way to find one is to check with your local, faster-growing churches.

Dating services do offer alternatives to meeting people, but they must be approached with caution. In *The Challenge of Being Single,* Marie Edwards and Eleanor Hoover observe that people tend to "stretch facts" when filling out questionnaires for a dating service. They do this not so much because they want to deceive, but because they are not aware of how "wishful thinking" has become reality for them. Edwards and Hoover also warn that "many computer dating services use no electronic equipment whatsoever, there are too few clients and too few variables for anything but rudimentary matching that can better be done by hand."[3] There are some obvious advantages to dating services, but the chances of getting matched with a Christian person like yourself are pretty slim. If you decide to take this route, investigate the claims of the dating service very carefully. Ask for referrals and call other customers to see whether they were satisfied with the service.

In addition to the ways of meeting people we've listed here, we also recommend that you share with current friends your desire to meet new people. Your friends might introduce you to someone new, and a good friendship could result. Choose the friends you confide in with caution, though. Too many embarrassing situations—and catastrophic blind dates—have resulted from the overzealousness of friends "just trying to help."

We hope some of these ideas have motivated you to get out and meet new people. Sometimes it is difficult, especially if you are entering the dating scene again after divorce or the death of a spouse. But it is worth it to try.

Once you get to a place where there are people to meet, you have to start looking around for likely candidates. And then you have to start a conversation with them.

Oh no! What are you going to say?!

8.

Striking Up a Conversation

You walk into a room. After looking around for a few minutes, you spot someone standing by the snack tray. He looks available. He nods courteously to a few passersby, but he doesn't really look like he's "with" anyone. "I've got nothing to lose by walking over there and introducing myself," you say under your breath. "All he can do is walk away. No big deal, eh?" You decide to take a positive approach. You *will* walk over there, and he *will* want to talk to you. You're ready to walk across the room and say....

... Oh no! What will you say? It better be good. Those first words are critically important. They spell the difference between a friendship and a rejection.

What to say? ...

... what to say? ..

We've all had experiences like that. There has been someone we've wanted to meet and talk to. Only a few feet separated us, but that separation seemed like the Grand Canyon. Our first words could bridge that gulf, but we struggled to find the "right" words to say so we wouldn't sound illiterate or foolish.

This is a common situation, since few of us have been given the gift of starting and sustaining meaningful conversations. Most of the best conversationalists you've met have probably worked hard to develop their skill.

You can be a good conversationalist, too, if you are willing to put in some effort. Here are some tips to help you:

(1) *Be approachable.* Don't stay in "packs" with several other people because doing so might scare off those who would like to start a conversation with you. If you are lost in a group of people, few others will be brave enough to come into the group and single you out. Make use of nonverbal communication—

facial expressions, stance, and bearing—to tell people you're open to talking with them. Try to maintain an open stance instead of folding your arms across your chest. Keep your hands and arms free to move and gesture.

(2) *Be positive.* Smile. Be excited about yourself and about life. We don't necessarily mean you fake a bubbly, exuberant personality—especially if you are really a quiet type. But be upbeat and positive. A friend of ours, commenting on what she feels are important characteristics, told us:

> Be excited when talking about yourself. If you seem to be blasé about yourself and your life, you ruin the excitement in your listener. This turns them off and makes you seem snobbish. And it doesn't take a spectacular story to excite someone else! I have a friend who can make a trip to the Laundromat sound adventuresome just because she is keen to God's hand in her life and can recognize lessons in everyday events. I find myself eager to hear about her weekends because I can relate to her life and experiences. She doesn't have to put me into a fantasy world of the unbelievable to make me want to know more about her.

(3) *Wear a conversation piece.* This idea is for the more adventurous! But an unusual piece of jewelry or a distinctive hat just might attract someone's attention and provide a subject for conversation—as long as your "conversation piece" is in good taste. "Wear a lapel pin with a message printed on it," says Helen Gurley Brown, editor of *Cosmopolitan.* "I have three. One says, 'I have grey hair, brown eyes, and a black heart,' and it has always been a smash hit. Once people see writing on you, they won't rest until they've read it. Total strangers will put on glasses to make the grade, and after that they almost have to say something to you not to be rude."[1]

(4) When you make contact with someone—either by catching their eye, smiling, or sitting next to them—*begin by introducing yourself.* You might also want to make a brief statement about who you are. Quite often this opener will be in the context of the situation in which you are meeting:

—"Hi. I'm Joan. This is my second time at worship here. It's really great, isn't it?"

—"Hi. I'm Steve. This is an interesting party, don't you think?"

(5) *Try giving the other person a compliment:*
  —"I like your dress. That color is just great on you."
  —"You're really tan for this time of year. Do you ski?"
(6) *If it is appropriate for the context, ask for help.*
  —"This is awfully heavy. Can you help me carry it to the car?"
  —"I seem to have left my bleach at home. Can I borrow a little bit of yours?"
(7) *Try some self-disclosure:*
  —"I'm really intimidated at parties like this. I wonder if I'm the only person who feels out of place."
  —"Gee, that was a great sermon. I needed to be reminded to reach out more to other people. We singles sometimes get rather selfish, don't we?"
(8) *If in a bind, try some clichés!*
  —"This weather is incredible. Can you ever remember it being so hot (cold)?"
  —"I haven't seen you before. Are you new here?"
(9) *Express an interest in another person's expertise.*
  —"How did you become such a good tennis player?"
  —"I hear you own your own business. How did you get started?"

While the key to *starting* a conversation is to appear interesting and open, the most important way to *keep* it going is to listen. By listening, we mean not only hearing the words spoken by the person you've met, but reading their nonverbal cues as well. Look for interest in their eyes, in their stance, in any gestures of openness they might exhibit as you make your first approach.

Kenny's Comments:
  Being able to listen is vitally important to keeping a conversation going. Listening, in fact, is one of the most important aspects of keeping a whole friendship alive.
  I have a friend, Priscilla, who has a knack for making people feel comfortable and loved almost from the moment she meets them. She is a physical education teacher at the University of Texas and is not a "raving beauty." Nor is she bubbling or outgoing. But men who have been attracted to her say there is a

*quality about her that is very appealing. They vaguely define it
as an ability to make them feel that she really cares about them.*

*While talking to her one time, I tried to key in on what it is about
her that makes people feel so good. I noticed that whenever I was
with her I did most of the talking. She seemed to care about me
and what I felt and what I was doing. Second, many of her
remarks consisted of short questions, or short replies like
"Really?" "Wow," "That's great," or "Ummmm." Her short ex-
clamations helped keep the conversation flowing, and gave me
feedback and encouragement to keep on talking. Her smiles and
open stance let me know she was listening.*

*As a sincere person who knows the value of listening, Priscilla
has found the key to being a good conversationalist. And let me
hasten to add that, when the time is appropriate, she is also open
about talking of her own feelings and needs. That also helps a
conversation flow because her confidence in me as a friend helps
cement our friendship.*

Even in the best of circumstances, conversations end. Occasionally we might feel they have ended too soon. We want to
know more about a person and take more time to get to know
them. What's needed is an agreement to get together again. We
need a date.

9.

Getting Together: How to Ask and Be Asked for Dates

Getting together with people through dating can be a special time of enjoyment and personal growth. But too often people pass up opportunities to date. A common complaint within some Christian circles is that the men don't ask the women out. But men also complain that, when they do ask, they are often turned down.

The dating scene is complicated by the shyness some people feel around the opposite sex, by the difficulties some have adjusting to a newly divorced or widowed state, by the preoccupation of some with sexual needs and performances. Some singles have been "burned" by previous negative experiences; others are simply afraid to take risks. And some rate potential dates by such unrealistic standards that they disqualify many people whose presence in their lives could be a real blessing!

Whatever might be standing in the way of your fulfillment in dating, we ask you to face these constrictions head on. Reaching out is risky. You may get turned down or feel rejected. And we're not suggesting that you go out with everyone who asks you, or that you ask everyone who shows interest in you. It is important to make dating "quality time" by spending it with those with whom you can share ideas as well as enjoy social engagements.

One word of advice: if you have problems that are giving you a negative attitude about dating, we suggest that you go to the Lord with these before you try to revitalize your dating life. This is because a negative attitude produces negative responses in others. And a negative attitude can't be hidden for long; if you harbor feelings of inadequacy or fear of the opposite sex, for example, sooner or later your voice, words, or actions will give you away. One of the greatest instigators of negative attitudes is the fear of rejection. Dr. David Viscott, author of *Risking,* warns that "expecting rejection only fills you with fear, and makes you act as the least desirable version of yourself, causing you to make other people uncomfortable."

So, if you have fears of rejection or anything else that causes you to be less than your best in a dating situation, ask God to help you change. "But why should it matter to God how I feel about dating?" you may ask. Well, 2 Timothy 1:7 provides an answer: "The Holy Spirit, God's gift, does not want you to be afraid of people, but to be wise and strong, and to love them and enjoy being with them" (TLB). It is obvious that God wants your positive attitude to generate positive results in every kind of relationship. That includes dating.

Another thing: often you can tell before you ask whether a person is interested in you. But sometimes you have no indication until you ask—or they ask you. Therefore it's natural that you will have some disappointment. However, if you get turned down often, or if your expressions of interest are continually rejected, then it is time to reassess what you are doing. And again, the best place to start is in prayer with God.

Asking Someone for a Date

The following guidlines may be "old hat" to some and new to others. They are the "basics" for asking someone for a date. We encourage you to read them and put them into practice. And enjoy yourself!

(1) When you make contact with the person—either by phone or in person—*identify yourself fully,* unless you are absolutely sure he or she will remember you. It is better to give your first and last name than to embarrass yourself and the other person by forcing him or her to say, "Andy who?" or "Mary who?"

(2) *Make a link between the past and present* so he or she can remember you. Or, make some kind of comment that will let them know how you came to meet each other.

(3) In general, we suggest you *don't get involved in a lot of small talk* unless the other person initiates it. Get to the point of asking the person for the date. Then, if he or she seems open to talk, by all means continue.

(4) *Be specific about the invitation.* It's in poor taste to ask a

person out for the first time and then to ask what he or she would like to do. That person has no idea what your budget is or what you may have had in mind. So don't place them in an awkward position. Have something planned before you ask.

(5) *Don't pressure the person into making a commitment.* If he or she seems hesitant, or if they say the date is not convenient, ask if an alternative time would be better. If the answer is still no, or he or she makes evasive comments (which in essence are saying no), then politely end the conversation and set your sights on someone else.

On Being Asked

Let's flip the coin now and talk about what to do when you are the one who is asked out. Many of us aren't quite sure how to respond. Here are a few hints:

(1) If the invitation is not to your liking, but you want to go out with the person, then make an *alternative suggestion.* For example: "I think it would be great to get together, but I'm uncomfortable going to "R"-rated movies. I'd like to do something else, though."

(2) Generally, *avoid the trap of answering the question, "What are you doing Saturday night?" directly.* Attempt to get the person to commit to what he or she has in mind. You might respond, "I'm not sure. What do you have in mind?"

(3) *If you are unable to go out when you are invited, but you would like to see the person another time, tell him or her.* You might say, "I've already made plans for that evening. But another time would be great."

(4) *If you don't want to go out with someone, say so.* It is unkind to "string someone along" with excuses and give that person false hope simply because you don't want to hurt his or her feelings. The most courteous response is to be honest with the person initially. Decline as graciously as possible, however, allowing the person to "save face." A possible response is, "Thanks, but I'd really rather not. I appreciate your asking, though."

Remember, you are the person being asked. You have the right to say yes or no. But you also have an obligation to the other person's feelings. Always be kind, even if the request is coming from a person you would never consider dating.

Should a Woman Ask Out a Man?

As you've probably noticed, in giving these guidelines we've avoided making the man the "asker" and the woman the "askee." Some women feel comfortable suggesting a date to a man. And, as social customs change in our society, more and more men feel comfortable being asked.

Yet we suspect the majority of you still feel more at ease with the traditional custom of men asking women. When you first meet someone it is hard to determine what their feelings might be about this matter. So generally, women, we advise caution. The majority of men aren't completely liberated yet, and they often will feel threatened by a female asserting herself in this role.

Kenny's Comments:

When people ask me how I feel about women asking out men, I have to answer with "it depends." I enjoy being asked out by female friends or women I've already asked out. In each case, my degree of comfort or discomfort rests on the nature of our friendship. If a female friend, a "sister," asks, I feel comfortable because I know we will have a pleasant, platonic evening. No romantic expectations—just friendship. Our relationship is defined, and we both know it. Also, when a woman I've dated some says, "Let's go to a show Saturday night," that is also comfortable. Again, our relationship is defined and I know she feels comfortable suggesting activities to me.

It feels uncomfortable for me—and for most men I suspect— when a total, or near-total, stranger asks me out. I'm not sure what she has in mind, so I'm a little defensive. It depends on the person, but I imagine most men would like to know where the woman stands. (I know most of you women would appreciate knowing where a man stands when he asks you out, too.) Women, you could do us men a big favor (by teaching us how to be more specific about asking) if, when you asked us out, you let it be known that you "just wanted to get together and get to know each other better." And it would be helpful to keep the date as informal as possible.

Basically, ladies, there aren't any hard and fast rules for this new, evolving situation. Common sense and open communication should be the general guidelines. But one thing to keep in

mind is that few men are ready for women to completely take
over their role as the "asker." Therefore, it is usually not in the
woman's best interests to ask a man who is a new acquaintance
for some kind of typically romantic date.

But you can certainly be creative and capture his interests
with a casual date! You might invite him to drive over to your
place for a Saturday morning car wash. Organize all the
equipment together and do both your cars. Follow up with
brunch. Or challenge the man to a game of tennis, or Par-
cheesi, or chess at your place, and then serve cookies. Or invite
him for a Saturday afternoon bike ride or picnic. Let your creative juices flow. You can come up with some ideas, suited for
the man you'd like to get to know, that are casual and not
threatening to his role.

What to Do?

For both men and women, the success of your first date can
depend on what you decide to do. In our society, there are a lim-
itless number of activities people can do together. Sometimes,
though, we get into a rut with the standard dating activity
of dinner and a movie. It's exciting to do something different. For instance, you could attend a soccer or basketball
game, go jogging, take a walk on the beach, or share a picnic in
the park. Museums, art shows, swap meets, or antique parlors
can be fun and fascinating—or you could spend the day exploring a nearby tourist town. Try going to the zoo, flying a kite,
attending a special lecture, or going shopping. Or do something
you've never done before! Use your imagination, and you can
come up with a variety of fun activities the two of you can
enjoy.

In concluding this section, we want to add one final thought.
God plays a part in helping us meet and get together with
people. If we pray about meeting others, God will give us wisdom and help. He might give us something creative to say to
someone we are just meeting. He might give us a unique idea
for a date that will be just the kind of activity the other person
likes. Ultimately, he gives us the best friends that we have in
our lives. They are a part of the many wonderful gifts that he

gives. That is why we believe it is wise to consult him when asking for or accepting dates.

Getting a date usually only takes a few minutes. We ask, and the other person says yes or no. Making that date a success is quite another issue—one that requires still more creativity. . . .

10.

First Date Success

Have you ever stumbled over your words, spilled your water, stepped on someone's foot, or laughed too long at a joke? Perhaps the occasion was a first date. Why is it that first dates make us feel so nervous? Probably because we attach a great deal of importance to that first time out. We're uneasy about what our date will think of us. Are we interesting? Are we fun and entertaining? Are we appealing?

First dates can be compared to job interviews. Many of us really want to impress the person we're with. This is a situation in which all aspects of our being—our intellect, personality, financial assets, sex appeal, education, success, taste in clothes, manners, relationship with Christ—all add up for evaluation at the same time.

In the back of our mind, always, is the possibility that we won't be appealing—that we'll be rejected. We get excited and scared at the same time. We begin to wonder: "Is this the beginning of the courtship that will lead to marriage?" while at the same time thinking, "What if he (she) doesn't like me?" It's a unique situation, for we are evaluating as well as being evaluated. No wonder so many of us get the jitters!

Here are a few others tidbits of advice to help that first date become less tense:

(1) *Relax*. Social psychologists have found that it is an easygoing, relaxed attitude that most attracts the opposite sex. In fact, it counts more than money, good looks, or personality. How can we relax? First of all, we can ask God to help us. If we're prepared—doing all we can physically, spiritually, and mentally—we'll find it easier to relax.

And it helps to remember that the other person is probably as nervous as we are. We all have times when we feel insecure or intimidated by others. Often people who look like they have it all together are really nervous inside. In fact, some people act "cool" just to hide their insecurity. No one ever "completely arrives."

Cherie's Comments:

I met Don in the jacuzzi at the recreation club. Earlier, the bright red of his swimming trunks had caught my eye as I noticed him walking toward the pool. I had thought he might be an athletic coach, since he had such a good build and well-toned body. I had wondered if he was single, and decided I'd like to meet him if he was.

The next thing I knew, he had seated himself beside me and started a conversation. We talked till we almost passed out from the heat. Finally, he asked if he could see me later that evening.

I discovered he was a natural at keeping the conversation flowing. We talked our way through the night—or I should say I mostly talked through the night. He was so good at encouraging me to talk that I can't remember when I'd chatted so much about myself.

Before he left, we made a dinner date for the next Friday night, which pleased me. But the more I thought about it, the more nervous I got. He was so cool about everything. He was great at asking questions and really listening to me. But I felt that I'd talked myself out already, and I'd asked him all the questions I could think of on that first night. I knew I couldn't expect him to keep the conversation going all the time. I wondered if there would be anything left to say on Friday, or if our dinner would be eaten in awkward silence.

Well, my fears were unwarranted. He kept talking all the way through dinner. In fact, we enjoyed a good conversation on that night, just as we have on many other dates. So you can imagine my surprise when he told me, several months later, that he too had been nervous about our first date, and had felt a little intimidated by me.

One of the best ways to become at ease on a date is to stop thinking about your nervousness. Concentrate on ways to make your date feel at ease. Get him or her to talk, to laugh and always remember to listen. Think of ways to have fun.

When you get your mind off yourself, you'll find your tension is lessened.

(2) *Be positive.* Expect to have a good time. If you project failure, you'll probably get it. But if you expect to have a good time, you'll be more relaxed and able to enjoy and contribute to the evening. Your date may not result in a great, long-term relationship, but it can be a good opportunity for getting to know another person. It's an educational as well as social experience, and you can welcome the opportunity.

If things go wrong, don't be a complainer. Don't grumble about the food, the poor seats, your aching feet, or the loud music. In almost every instance, the person who made the arrangements for the evening had nothing to do with the circumstances. Don't embarrass or annoy him or her by dwelling on the negative aspects of the date. Even if you made the arrangements, don't be critical; complaining will only put a damper on the evening. Instead, make the most of the situation, and look at any annoyances as opportunities to make a joke, or to display your tolerance and patience—traits most people find appealing.

(3) *Plan, but allow for spontaneity.* In the previous chapter, we talked about the importance of planning a date. Questions like "What would you like to do this evening?" or "Where would you like to go for dinner?" are almost always death blows to a first date. Once you have a relationship established, those are fine questions to ask. But the first date should be planned.

At the same time, you don't want to *over*plan; that's why we recommend some spontaneity. It's exciting to have an element of surprise, to be able to enjoy some creativity on the date.

Cherie's Comments:
I had a date surprise me once after dinner by suggesting we drive to a house that he had sold for a client that day. It had a spectacular view of the valley. I enjoyed the drive. And running up a winding, moonlit driveway was definitely romantic, as was the view of the city lights from the windy hill. But what made his idea the most fun was that it was different; it was an unexpected pleasure—like receiving a little gift for no particular reason.

(4) *Look for opportunities for fun and lightheartedness.* As Christians we might think dating should have its serious side. And that's true; we have a whole realm of conversational possibilities that non-Christians don't have—we can share our relationship with Jesus. But we also have the freedom to be "crazy"! So share a talent or have a sing-along while on your date. Go ahead and walk in the rain! Who cares if you race to the car after dinner? Dare to let the child in you come out on your date. If you go out expecting to be entertained, and not doing much to liven up the evening yourself, you'll contribute little to pleasant memories. So allow yourself the freedom to do something unusual or silly, as long as it's in good taste.

(5) *Get involved in what your date has planned for the time together.* If you go to a party, don't be the one to pooh-pooh the idea of charades. So what if you feel a little self-conscious? Someone else does, too. Try to participate in what has been planned. If you have a good reason not to (health, conflict with your Christian principles, etc.), then explain your situation as politely as possible. Maybe you can even offer an alternative suggestion.

(6) *Unless you are going Dutch Treat, let your date entertain you the way he or she wants to.* If you are taken to a good restaurant or to an expensive play, don't respond with "Oh, I think that's too expensive," or "Why are you spending all that money on me?" On the other hand, don't expect your dates to take you to expensive places; they don't owe it to you. And, if they do treat you to a high-priced evening, you don't owe them anything in return. Especially sexual favors.

(7) *Be on time.* Being late is one of the most impolite things you can do on a first date. The only thing that is worse is not showing up at all. If you are running late, it is courteous to call and inform your date. It is no longer fashionable to "keep a man waiting" by being a half hour late; likewise, men who arrive late for a date are saying something about themselves that needs to be carefully examined.

(8) *Be interested.* The first date is a time to get to know each other. So be prepared to ask questions, the type of questions we've discussed as helping conversation along. At the same time, be sensitive to areas the other person might not like to

disclose, and steer clear of any really personal questions unless your date begins to volunteer information in that area.

(9) *Don't use the date as a "dumping ground."* The first date is a time to get to know another person—not to dump all your frustrations on him or her. It is fine to divulge information about yourself, but it is generally wise to steer clear of long conversations about past relationships. And avoid derogatory comments about your former dates or mates. There will be time later to share in depth if you continue to see each other.

(10) *Be objective and open to new ideas.* Wait until you've gotten to know someone before you close your mind to him or her. Some people spend an entire evening mentally picking the other person apart. If you find your date to be something other than what you anticipated, give him or her a chance. Anybody can have a bad day and put their worst foot forward. Don't be quick to judge; use the date as a time to listen to new ideas and get acquainted with a different type of personality.

(11) *Don't apologize for yourself.* Don't run down your old Volkswagen, your new haircut, or your clothes, and don't spend the time worrying about how you look. Some people are obsessed with running themselves down; others are continually running to a mirror. Neither trait is intriguing. Now, we're not saying you can't ever make a comment about yourself, or poke fun at your old rattletrap of a car, or check yourself out in a mirror. Actually, it's a good idea to excuse yourself after dinner to make sure a piece of lettuce isn't hanging from a tooth! And many couples have had a lot of fun laughing about situations that could have otherwise been awkward. But the point is: worrying about how you're coming across won't change a thing, except show your date how insecure you are.

(12) *Dress appropriately.* We've already discussed dress. But make sure you find out what type of occasion your date will be and then dress appropriately. If you aren't sure, ask your date for advice.

(13) *Don't be pressured into kissing or other physical involvement.* If you do go out with someone who is overeager on the first date, make your point gently but firmly. Don't trap yourself into any kind of physical expression simply because you are afraid this person will never go out with you again if you don't. Actually, if you are not true to yourself and your

eone who unceremoniously used
ed this all up by saying, "I can't
e-scarred than the soul of a single

can be healed through the power
begin to change this philosophy
own "game plan." This means
erson we date as a friend rather
r our own gratification. It means
up, to help them become all *God*
es the desire to share our lives,
H. Roper. "And it will cost! It will
ul. This, then, is the secret of
lain:

which occurs on my behalf, some-
friend is someone to whom I give,
e with, so that they come to a full
as planned for them. That is what
g. It will involve teaching. It will
ion. . . . It will involve the bearing
life.[1]

dating we've found is Matthew
thyself" (KJV). Though the Bible
s for dating, it is rich in advice
te to each other. Here are nine-
friends should treat each other:
son first. They consider the feel-
as well as their own. They don't
s with flirtatious promises they
honest and considerate. "Let no
t of his neighbor" (1 Cor. 10:24,

another. They don't wait for
their dates to make *them* feel
age their friends. Kind words of
gement, cost us nothing, yet we
em. "Let's please the other fel-
t is for his good and thus build
2, TLB).

moral responsibilities, it's likely that you'll feel bad about yourself and that this will ruin the future of your relationship. People worth seeing again will be impressed with your "no," not turned off by it. A date who expresses anger at your refusal or tries to "sweet talk" you into bed isn't for you; this type of person is selfish and interested only in his or her own gratification. Show respect for yourself, and others will, too.

(14) *Bring Jesus with you.* It may not be appropriate for you and your date to pray or share a great deal about Christianity on your first date. If it is, then by all means do so. But keep in mind always that God is with you in everything that you do; his love rests with you even on your nervous first date. Ask his blessing on your date, and ask him to help you make it an encouraging time. You may not go out with this person again, but you will have grown and learned, and God will turn that into something positive. If a relationship does develop, it will have a much stronger foundation because you prayed about it from the very beginning.

We hope your date is a success. We hope it results in a lifelong friendship. Speaking of friends, we noted earlier that God doesn't give any direct guidelines about dating. But he has lots to say about friendships.

11.

How to Win at the Dating Game

Do you want to win at the dating game? You can. But not by using the world's standards. Christians win at the dating game by doing away with games. Instead, we win by using the fruits-of-the-spirit standard—exhibiting "love, joy, peace, patience, kindness, goodness, faithfulness, gentleness and self-control ... " (Gal. 5:22,23, TLB). And that means we treat each person we date as a very special friend.

Traditionally, our culture has not encouraged us to think of dating in terms of friendship. As we discussed earlier, Western culture has often taught us to practice deception and manipulation in romantic relationships. We have been conditioned to see our dates as objects that should excite us with feelings of euphoria and passion. They are supposed to make us feel better about ourselves. But such practices and attitudes are selfish and counterproductive. They actually wreck relationships. And they alienate the sexes.

Cherie's Comments:

A conversation I had with a friend well illustrates this popular but subversive philosophy. Seated on the couch one afternoon, I listened at length to my friend discuss her romantic problems. One man cared for her a great deal; she kept him "on the string" as a kind of insurance against loneliness. Most of her time, however, was devoted to another man who was less devoted to her, but who intrigued her. Since his interest in her had waned slightly, she had decided she really wanted him.

"Why is it," I wondered, "that we usually want what we can't have?"

She continued discussing the man she wanted most. Lately he hadn't treated her right. They had had an argument over

someone they cared for—sor them. A friend of ours summ think of anything more battl person."

Thankfully our battle scars of the Holy Spirit. And we ca of dating by scrutinizing ou that we choose to see each p than as an object to exploit fo that we choose to build others wants them to be. "This tak whatever it costs," says David cost the giving up of our s friendship." He goes on to ex

Friendship is not something thing someone extends to me. A someone I want to share my li realization of everything God l a friend is. It will involve givi involve exhortation and correc of burdens and the sharing of

The most helpful "law" of 19:19: "Love thy neighbor as does not provide specific rule about how people should rela teen Biblical principles for how

(1) *Friends put the other per* ings of the persons they date, seek to build up their own ego don't intend to keep. They are one seek his own good, but tha NAS).

(2) *Friends encourage one* praises and compliments from good. They seek ways to encou praise, of sympathy, of encoura often refrain from speaking th low, not ourselves, and do wha him up in the Lord" (Rom. 15:

(3) *Friends honor each other.* They show respect for the other person's attitudes and feelings, even if they don't agree. They don't think of themselves as superior to their dates, but see them as equal in importance before God. "Love each other with brotherly affection and take delight in honoring each other" (Rom. 12:10, TLB).

(4) *Friends share each other's sorrows.* They are supportive of the people they date—not only during times of fun, but also when the going is difficult. They don't fade out of the picture when the other person is suffering emotionally, is physically ill, or has other problems. In fact, it is during the difficult times that a true friend offers comfort and support. "Share each other's troubles and problems, and so obey our Lord's command" (Gal. 6:2, TLB).

(5) *Friends rejoice together.* They choose to kick jealousy and possessiveness out of their lives. Even if a date's happy news does not seem in our best interest (such as when they may receive a job transfer requiring them to move), we should still be happy with them. "When others are happy, be happy with them" (Rom. 12:15, TLB).

(6) *Friends are honest with each other.* They don't manipulate or lie to the people they date. They are discreetly honest about their feelings towards each other. They give honest replies rather than false hope. "Stop lying to each other; tell the truth, for we are parts of each other and when we lie to each other we are hurting ourselves" (Eph. 4:25, TLB).

(7) *Friends are humble, gentle, and patient.* They are not critical, boastful, pushy, or rude. They seek to build the other person up. They don't boast of their own achievements. They don't put the other person down for not doing the same as they do. "Be humble and gentle. Be patient with each other, making allowance for each other's faults because of your love" (Eph. 4:2, TLB).

(8) *Friends are at peace with each other.* Friends have disagreements and even confrontations. But they don't engage in selfish quarreling and bickering. They are willing to discuss a situation which is annoying or hurtful. They choose to confront the problem at the time it is recognized, or pray for an opportune time to discuss it. "Don't quarrel with anyone. Be at peace with everyone, just as much as possible" (Rom. 12:18, TLB).

(9) *Friends don't stay angry with each other*. Instead of brooding over a situation that made them angry, they seek to understand what caused it. They'll make the time to discuss the situation, and seek to restore the friendship. "If you are angry, don't sin by nursing your grudge. Don't let the sun go down with you still angry—get it over quickly; for when you are angry you give a mighty foothold to the devil" (Eph. 4:26,27, TLB).

(10) *Friends forgive and ask for forgiveness*. No matter how right we are, or think we are, we are admonished to forgive. That doesn't mean we must necessarily condone the actions of our friends. It does mean that we choose to forgive, to start anew. And when we are wrong, we need to ask the other person to forgive us (*Matt*. 5:23, 24). Many times, both parties need to share in the blame and ask forgiveness of each other. "Be gentle and ready to forgive; never hold grudges. Remember, the Lord forgave you, so you must forgive others" (Col. 3:13, TLB).

(11) *Friends admit faults to each other*. This doesn't mean that friends need to adopt a "tell all" attitude, but that they should be open to share weaknesses when it is appropriate. In disclosing some of our weak points, we open the door to new levels of communication, and we give our friends the knowledge of how to pray for us. "Admit your faults to one another and pray for each other so that you may be healed. The earnest prayer of a righteous man has great power and wonderful results" (James 5:16, TLB).

(12) *Friends have pure thoughts about each other*. Planning ways to make someone "suffer" or make them jealous, scheming and devising plans to "get even" aren't examples of pure thoughts. Rather, we should be thinking of how to help our friends grow closer to God. "Treat . . . the girls [guys] as your sisters [brothers], thinking only pure thoughts about them (1 Tim. 5:2, TLB).

(13) *Friends don't criticize each other*. They choose to speak well of the people they date, or not to say anything at all. (Discussing a dating situation with a trusted friend and making honest statements is not what we're talking about.) The best action, aside from talking with trusted friends, is to take the matter to God in prayer. Pray that our friends will change, and then lovingly bring any unpleasant attitudes or behavior

moral responsibilities, it's likely that you'll feel bad about yourself and that this will ruin the future of your relationship. People worth seeing again will be impressed with your "no," not turned off by it. A date who expresses anger at your refusal or tries to "sweet talk" you into bed isn't for you; this type of person is selfish and interested only in his or her own gratification. Show respect for yourself, and others will, too.

(14) *Bring Jesus with you.* It may not be appropriate for you and your date to pray or share a great deal about Christianity on your first date. If it is, then by all means do so. But keep in mind always that God is with you in everything that you do; his love rests with you even on your nervous first date. Ask his blessing on your date, and ask him to help you make it an encouraging time. You may not go out with this person again, but you will have grown and learned, and God will turn that into something positive. If a relationship does develop, it will have a much stronger foundation because you prayed about it from the very beginning.

We hope your date is a success. We hope it results in a lifelong friendship. Speaking of friends, we noted earlier that God doesn't give any direct guidelines about dating. But he has lots to say about friendships.

11.

How to Win at the Dating Game

Do you want to win at the dating game? You can. But not by using the world's standards. Christians win at the dating game by doing away with games. Instead, we win by using the fruits-of-the-spirit standard—exhibiting "love, joy, peace, patience, kindness, goodness, faithfulness, gentleness and self-control . . . " (Gal. 5:22,23, TLB). And that means we treat each person we date as a very special friend.

Traditionally, our culture has not encouraged us to think of dating in terms of friendship. As we discussed earlier, Western culture has often taught us to practice deception and manipulation in romantic relationships. We have been conditioned to see our dates as objects that should excite us with feelings of euphoria and passion. They are supposed to make us feel better about ourselves. But such practices and attitudes are selfish and counterproductive. They actually wreck relationships. And they alienate the sexes.

Cherie's Comments:

A conversation I had with a friend well illustrates this popular but subversive philosophy. Seated on the couch one afternoon, I listened at length to my friend discuss her romantic problems. One man cared for her a great deal; she kept him "on the string" as a kind of insurance against loneliness. Most of her time, however, was devoted to another man who was less devoted to her, but who intrigued her. Since his interest in her had waned slightly, she had decided she really *wanted him.*

"Why is it," I wondered, "that we usually want what we can't have?"

She continued discussing the man she wanted most. Lately he hadn't treated her right. They had had an argument over something he had done or not done, and had parted on rather disgruntled terms. "I'm going to make him sweat it out!" she confided. "I'm just not going to be at home to receive his calls, should he try. I didn't go to the singles group at church today; he's probably wondering why I wasn't there. I'm not going to the committee meeting this week either. And I've already invited the other man to a party this weekend. So he can suffer a little!"

I just sat there. A relatively short time ago, I would have entered into the conversation with comments supportive of her actions. Subconsciously, my thoughts would have reflected past experiences when I'd been hurt or misunderstood by a man I had dated. I would have projected those feelings to the present situation. But my point of view was changing as I sat there. I had recognized some situations where I had misunderstood or hurt someone else. And the Lord had begun showing me how destructive that was. He helped me see beyond my own needs and pain.

As my friend talked further about the two men, I thought about them. "What are each of these men feeling right now?" I wondered. "What are their points of view, their frustrations, their hurts?" I knew the man who was currently the "bad guy" had his own story. I wished my friend would sit down with him and discuss her feelings rather than playing games and sending signals that neither of them understood very well. And I hoped she would be honest with the man who most wanted her affections and tell him what she was really feeling.

Before casting stones at Cherie's friend, let's admit that most of us have played games too. It's easy to do in dating. And most of us have been hurt by dating partners who played games with us. There's an old adage that says, "All's fair in love and war." Most of us will agree that nothing is fair about war. Is anything fair about inconsiderate or selfish behavior in dating? Most of us would say "no." But don't most of us still adhere to a philosophy of friendship that says, "Do whatever is necessary to win"?

Perhaps you've heard someone comment in anger, "Well, she (he) can just eat her (his) heart out." For some people this has become a reality. The hearts of scores of men and women have been "eaten out" by the unkind words and selfish actions of someone they cared for—someone who unceremoniously used them. A friend of ours summed this all up by saying, "I can't think of anything more battle-scarred than the soul of a single person."

Thankfully our battle scars can be healed through the power of the Holy Spirit. And we can begin to change this philosophy of dating by scrutinizing our own "game plan." This means that we choose to see each person we date as a friend rather than as an object to exploit for our own gratification. It means that we choose to build others up, to help them become all *God* wants them to be. "This takes the desire to share our lives, whatever it costs," says David H. Roper. "And it will cost! It will cost the giving up of our soul. This, then, is the secret of friendship." He goes on to explain:

> Friendship is not something which occurs on my behalf, something someone extends to me. A friend is someone to whom I give, someone I want to share my life with, so that they come to a full realization of everything God has planned for them. That is what a friend is. It will involve giving. It will involve teaching. It will involve exhortation and correction. . . . It will involve the bearing of burdens and the sharing of life.[1]

The most helpful "law" of dating we've found is Matthew 19:19: "Love thy neighbor as thyself" (KJV). Though the Bible does not provide specific rules for dating, it is rich in advice about how people should relate to each other. Here are nineteen Biblical principles for how friends should treat each other:

(1) *Friends put the other person first.* They consider the feelings of the persons they date, as well as their own. They don't seek to build up their own egos with flirtatious promises they don't intend to keep. They are honest and considerate. "Let no one seek his own good, but that of his neighbor" (1 Cor. 10:24, NAS).

(2) *Friends encourage one another.* They don't wait for praises and compliments from their dates to make *them* feel good. They seek ways to encourage their friends. Kind words of praise, of sympathy, of encouragement, cost us nothing, yet we often refrain from speaking them. "Let's please the other fellow, not ourselves, and do what is for his good and thus build him up in the Lord" (Rom. 15:2, TLB).

to their attention. "Don't criticize and speak evil about each other, dear brothers. If you do, you will be fighting against God's law of loving one another, declaring it is wrong" (James 4:11, TLB).

(14) *Friends don't lead each other into sin.* They are sensitive about suggesting anything that might tempt the other person to sin. And they won't put pressure on that person to commit a sexual act that is sinful. "The right thing to do is to quit eating meat or drinking wine or doing anything else that offends your brother or makes him sin" (Rom. 14:21, TLB).

(15) *Friends rely on God's wisdom.* They know that they will never be knowledgeable enough to keep a relationship going on their own. "I advise you to obey only the Holy Spirit's instructions. He will tell you where to go and what to do, and then you won't always be doing the wrong things your evil nature wants you to" (Gal. 5:16, TLB).

(16) *Friends keep their promises.* They don't break dates because someone better comes along. They are on time for dates. And they follow through with the things they offer to do. "God delights in those who keep their promises, and abhors those who don't" (Prov. 12:22, TLB).

(17) *Friends pray with each other.* They pray for those they date, and ask God's blessings on their lives. They pray for their friends' weak points, instead of criticizing them. "Pray all the time. Ask God for anything in line with the Holy Spirit's wishes. Plead with him, reminding him of your needs, and keep praying earnestly for all Christians everywhere" (Eph. 6:18, TLB).

(18) *Friends talk about God with each other.* Sharing new discoveries in the Lord gives a relationship a depth that is otherwise unattainable. And when we worship together, our hearts are united in a way that is lacking in other relationships. "Talk with each other much about the Lord, quoting psalms and hymns and singing sacred songs, making music in your hearts to the Lord (Eph. 5:19, TLB).

(19) *Friends treat each other as they want to be treated.* That sums it up, doesn't it? In every dating situation, friends act out of love. "You have been given freedom ... to love and serve each other. For the whole Law can be summed up in this one command: 'Love others as you love yourself'" (Gal. 5:13,14,TLB).

That's quite a list, isn't it? As you may have noticed, this list of friendship principles applies to the way we treat everyone we meet. So we want to suggest a little exercise. Begin practicing them with everyone you know. Then, when you are dating a special person, the principles will be all the easier to put into effect.

At this point, we imagine a few of you are saying, "But these apply when both people are Christians. What if a Christian is dating a non-Christian?" Or, more fundamentally, you may be asking, "Can a Christian date a non-Christian?" That's a good question. Our answer may surprise you.

12.

Can I Date Nonbelievers?

Step into most gatherings of single Christians and you'll find that one of the most-asked, most-discussed questions is: "Can a Christian date a non-Christian?"

And you'll find a variety of responses to this controversial question, including:

—"I was taught growing up in the church that Christians shouldn't date non-Christians. Non-Christians lead Christians away from God—especially if the relationship ends in marriage. A believer can't be 'unequally yoked' with a nonbeliever, God says. So we're not supposed to even date nonbelievers."

—"Sure, I know the Bible says we shouldn't be 'unequally yoked' with a nonbeliever. But it doesn't say we can't date them. Not all dating leads to marriage, you know. I can go out with a nonbeliever, have a good time, and still not want to be married."

—"Hey, let's be practical. There aren't any Christians where I work. And I never meet any eligible bachelors at church. I'm not desperate for a mate, anyway. So why not go out with a non-Christian?"

—"He loves me and I love him. He's not a Christian now, but after we're married, I'll work on him. You'll see."

Do any of these statements sound familiar? To be truthful, both of us have made comments similar to all four at various times in our lives. Yet, overall, our individual experiences differ greatly. Cherie has had many negative experiences dating nonbelievers; she counsels extreme caution to the point of saying it is rare that a Christian should date a non-Christian. Kenny's experiences have been more positive; he was led to the Lord through the ministry of several Christians he dated. So, while counseling caution, he feels that "mixed" dating is an opportunity for Christians to present a message of hope and comfort to hurting, searching people.

Our opinions, then, are quite personal. So are yours. So let's do away with the theoretical question, "Can a Christian date a non-Christian?" Let's ask a more personal question: "Should *you* date a nonbeliever?"

It Depends

Our answer is an unequivocal maybe! It depends on whether your relationship with Christ is strong enough, whether God has called you to this delicate form of ministry, and whether your date is scoffer or a seeker. We'll deal with each of these "whethers" in this chapter. But first, let's look at some of the reasons we think Christians should approach with caution the idea of dating nonbelievers.

In most conversations about dating non-Christians, the phrase, "do not be unequally yoked" is mentioned. The verse is found in 2 Corinthians 6:14–15:

> Be ye not unequally yoked together with unbelievers: for what fellowship hath righteousness with unrighteousness? and what communion hath light with darkness? And what concord hath Christ with Belial? or what part hath he that believeth with an infidel? (KJV)

The imagery of being unequally yoked comes from Deuteronomy 22:10, "Thou shalt not plough with an ox and ass together." Why not? Because the ox is much stronger and pulls along the helpless donkey as the two work the fields together. It's like a seven-foot behemoth putting his arms around you in a headlock and then pulling you down the street, your legs dangling so you only occasionally make contact with the sidewalk. You are at his mercy. That is how it is when a Christian and a non-Christian are "unequally yoked."

When applied to dating, as this verse often is, it is used to discourage dating between believers and nonbelievers. The advice is based on a fear that the believer and nonbeliever will fall in love and get married. This creates a marriage that is spiritually dangerous, with the nonbeliever dragging the believer around like an ox drags an ass. So traditionally church leaders have prescribed preventive medicine: "You can't marry a non-Christian, so don't take a chance on disaster by dating one."

We feel the traditional wisdom of the church is sound. And we'd even take the caution one step further. We think it's possible for a Christian to be unequally yoked with a Christian! This occurs when one Christian is not living according to God's will. These people are often called backsliders. Because they aren't living a Christian life, their influence can be just as corrupting as the influence of a person who has never given his or her life to God. So, for our purposes, when we say "unbeliever" we are referring to both non-Christians and backsliders.

Aside from the fact that Paul cautioned us against "mixed" marriages, there is another reason we counsel caution in dating nonbelievers. This second warning comes from our chapter on friendship. You'll note that biblical friendship rests strongly on the idea that true friends share, pray, and worship together. That's how we tap into the power of God to strengthen our relationships. If a nonbeliever and a believer are dating, this power is unavailable. Since we cannot commune with a nonbeliever about Jesus, we really have only half a relationship when we are dating them. The most important aspect of communication between us, our Christianity, is missing.

Are you Strong Enough?

Having laid this foundation, let's take a personal inventory. Do you think you are strong enough in your relationship with Christ to avoid being a "donkey?" If you think so, can you truthfully answer "yes" to these eleven questions?:

(1) Are you willing to do anything God asks—even deny yourself a "dream date"?

(2) Can you withstand criticism and ridicule for your Christian beliefs and still stand on your faith?

(3) Is your relationship with Christ so important that you wouldn't want to do anything to jeopardize it?

(4) Are you liberated from loneliness or depression as a motivation for dating?

(5) Are you a person of constant prayer, Bible study, and worship?

(6) Do you often pray about your relationships with others, seeking God's presence in every phase of those relations?

(7) Are you part of a cohesive community of believers—either a closely knit church group or a small Bible study group?

(8) Do you have a close friend of the same sex with whom you can honestly share your concerns?

(9) Are you by nature a strong-willed, self-confident person who is not overly impressed by good looks, money, or power?

(10) Are you by nature "other directed," caring more about others than about yourself?

(11) If a woman, are you willing to live a role reversal by being the leader of a relationship, steering it towards a constant consideration of the things of God?

If you can't answer "yes" to each of these questions, you run a high risk of being negatively influenced by your date rather than being a positive influence on him or her. If you answered "yes," then you *may* be called to minister to the unbeliever. But even if you do possess the necessary spiritual maturity, you must still pray fervently that God will reveal to you, by his Spirit, whether you have been called to date nonbelievers. If you don't, you may regret it.

Cherie's Comments:

I was raised in a loving Christian atmosphere. I was a youth leader at church and counseled kids not to date non-Christians. But I met a nonbeliever at work who really intrigued me. He asked me out, and I decided to say "yes." I figured I was strong enough in the Lord to withstand any temptation. I would share Jesus with him, I resolved.

But I found on our first date that he didn't want to talk about religion. He wanted to wine and dine me. And I loved the attention. It made me feel special. No Christian guy, I'm sorry to say, had made me feel so good about myself. Soon I saw that my resolve was not as strong as I thought. But I was having such a good time that I put my conscience in a mental closet and carried on.

After dating the first non-Christian guy, I dated others. They, too, had little use for religion, and I gave in to their desire not to talk about Jesus. My whole relationship with the Lord crumbled as I enjoyed the company of my nonbelieving dates.

The Lord's love for me never left, though. He kept chipping away at me until I became overwhelmed by guilt. My journey back into fellowship has not been an easy one, because the allure of dating some of these men remains strong. That is why I rarely date nonbelievers today. When I do, I make sure it is a casual date, and that my dates know beforehand of my Christian beliefs.

We hope Cherie's story emphasizes the caution that needs to be exercised when dating nonbelievers. She would have answered "yes" to most of the questions we posed. Yet she stumbled. That's the reason we said you need to possess not only spiritual maturity, but also a calling from God.

Dating as Evangelism

We feel that people who date non-Christians have a special ministry from God. The most important gift needed for such a ministry is that of evangelism. An evangelist is "one who announces good tidings" (see Eph. 4:11 and 2 Tim. 4:5). You may also possess the gifts of serving, teaching, and encouraging (Rom. 12:6–8), but you must first of all be filled with a self-sacrificing zeal to declare the message of Christ to all nations (see Matt. 28:18–20). The nations start with the people God puts into our lives. And some of these people may be those we date.

For those who have been called, and we hope by now you have a good idea of who you are, there can be many wonderful results from ministering to nonbelievers!

Kenny's Comments:

My sophomore year in college I began dating Marsha. I knew she was a Christian before I asked her out, but I didn't know how strong she really was. I grew up in the surfer culture, where having anything to do with religion was considered weakness. It was definitely "uncool" to need a religious crutch, I thought. But

*there was an emotional void in my life, a feeling of emptiness,
and I thought Marsha might have something to say about that.
Why was she a Christian, anyway? I wondered. I figured if she
wanted to talk about God, I would use her as a sounding board
for all my questions. So she patiently answered each of my
queries about Christians and Christianity.*

*It so happened that our parents lived in the same city, and we
would drive home on semester breaks. During those long hours
on the road, she began to show me that the Christian alternative
to life was one I should reconsider. She also encouraged me to
enroll in a Bible class in college. Finally, her patient witness
and my studies paid off: I gave my life to the Lord towards the
end of my sophomore year.*

*I know that the college scene is different from "real life." But
among the fifty people I know who have been saved through the
witness of a person they were dating, many were already working in the "real world." Since I graduated, I've had several opportunities to share the Lord with people at work. I don't make a
habit of dating nonbelievers, mind you, but when I have, the
experiences have been a good time for ministry.*

Scoffers and Seekers

Analyzing why our experiences are so varied led us to two
conclusions. One is that Cherie may have been less spiritually
mature at the time than was Marsha. But we think the more
compelling reason is that the attitudes of the guys Cherie
dated differed from the attitude Kenny possessed when he
began dating Marsha.

Cherie calls her dates "the scoffers." The term comes from 2
Peter 3:3: "First of all, you must understand that in the last
days scoffers will come, scoffing and following their own evil
desires" (NIV). Some visible traits of scoffers are:

(1) They'll be quick to impress you with superficialities such
as their looks, important friends, possessions, or wealth.

(2) They may make sly comments about sex, tell rude jokes,
or use bad language.

(3) They'll think nothing about wining and dining you at
dinner, taking you to an "R" or "X"-rated movie, and then
taking you home for sex.

(4) They make comments about "not needing a crutch," or they'll say that religion is passé.

(5) Their basic life philosophy can be summed up with the words of the rich man in Jesus' parable: "Eat, drink, and be merry."

No matter how spiritually mature you are, you'll fight a losing battle if you become involved with a scoffer. Their hearts are hardened. Their motives towards you can only result in disaster. Avoid them.

Seekers

There is another group of nonbelievers, however, who are different from the scoffers. Kenny was a seeker. He was open to new ideas. God had prepared his heart to receive the words of the people he dated. You can usually spot a seeker because they are curious about what makes you tick. Knowing you are a Christian, they are apt to seek you out. They may comment, "I don't know what you've got, but I'd sure like to have it for myself." When told you're a Christian, they'll likely respond, "That's interesting. I'd like to talk to you more about that sometime."

David was such a seeker. He had moved from the East Coast to California due to a job transfer. Seeking to meet new friends, he attended a church social recommended by an acquaintance. He met Noelle at a volleyball game. At the time she was dating a Christian, but she was attracted to David's sensitivity and honesty. David picks up the narrative at this point:

> I prayed the Lord's prayer every day growing up, and I considered myself a Christian. But I really didn't know the concept of being born again. When I began dating Noelle, we talked about this difference. She helped me realize the disparity between the Christian and the non-Christian walk. That difference was a definite stumbling block early in our relationship. I said I always wanted to date women with strong religious beliefs, but I never thought those beliefs would so strongly affect our relationship.
>
> I didn't want to make any commitments just to appease Noelle or to manipulate her into spending more time with me. So I started studying Christianity by myself. I talked with other Christians. I read *Born Again* by Charles Colson and books by

C. S. Lewis and Josh McDowell. I found my confusion related more
to having never heard the complete gospel message than to being
a person of no faith. Since I gave myself to Jesus, there have been
some remarkable changes in my relationship with Noelle. It is as
if a whole new dimension of our lives was opened up.

Strategies for Seed Planters

In telling about these "successes," we've touched on some
strategies you may use to minister through dating. Let's
enumerate them:

(1) *You are expected to exercise spiritual leadership.* You
must see to it that your behavior is in keeping with the Lord's
desires for Christian living. Let your "good deeds glow for all to
see, so that they will praise your heavenly Father" (Matt. 5:16,
TLB). It is your task to plant seeds. You may or may not see the
harvest.

(2) *Carefully consider dating requests.* Women, we don't
think it is being too naïve to tell a man you'll need a day or two
to think and pray about a dating request. If he still wants to
date you after you've submitted his request to God, then
chances are your Christianity is of interest to him.

Susan, an Inter-Varsity Christian Fellowship leader, remem-
bers a dating opportunity she refused. "He asked me to see an
"R"-rated movie. I didn't think it would be uplifting to me. So I
told him "no," and then explained why I wouldn't go to that
show. I said I'd be glad to go out with him someplace else. He
responded to my honesty with pleasant surprise. I gained much
respect from him because of my stand." If a man is sensitive to
you, he will suggest dating activities that are nonoffensive and
comfortable. He won't create a situation destined to bring
moral and ethical conflict.

Men—you, too, have a responsiblity. Plan dates with non-
Christian women that allow time for discussion. You are God's
representative in this situation, and how you act may make an
eternal difference in the life of the woman you're dating.

(3) *Keep a platonic attitude* about dating nonbelievers. Make
the dates informal. Avoid places where romantic feelings or
sexual arousal can occur.

(4) *Be spiritually prepared for your date.* Pray that God will

bless your actions. And pray that he will create an open mind in your date. Pray also that an opportunity to talk about your beliefs will occur.

"I don't think it is too naïve to believe that if God is all powerful he will create a situation in which you will have the opportunity to talk about your faith," Susan says. Noelle says that every time she prayed about a date, God answered her prayer. "Every time I've gone out with a nonbeliever, one of us has brought up the subject of my faith, and the conversation has been quite comfortable. I've never feared that I would not have a chance to witness. If you pray, the opportunity will arise. If the guy is interested in you, he will ask to know more about Jesus, because he will see how important God is in your life."

(5) If your date has any interest in Christianity, *encourage—but don't pressure—him or her to study God's word and seek the advice and friendship of other believers.* When David questioned Noelle, she directed him to a pastor. She also gave him books to read that expanded on those he had already studied. "I've found that a Bible study on Jesus is quite an eye-opener to most nonbelievers," Susan says. "Most I've talked to say Christians preach one thing and do another. I usually have to admit to my date that this is sometimes true, but that even if some Christians are unattractive, their leader certainly is not. I explain that it is Jesus who should be emulated. And then I either lead a study or direct him to an ongoing study where Jesus is taught as a compassionate and courageous person. Most nonbelievers respond favorably when Jesus is presented in this light."

Setting a Deadline

The longer you date a nonbeliever, the more likely it is that a romantic relationship will develop. Some Christians say that when they begin dating a nonbeliever they set a deadline with the Lord. "I put conditions on my friendship with David," Noelle recalls. "I didn't tell David, but I did pray to the Lord about it a lot. I felt that if David did not appear to be drawing closer to God by the end of the summer, then I'd ask that our relationship be redefined. I was even prepared to break up."

Noelle says that she could have coped with some emotional attachment to David, but that a complete romantic involvement would have been damaging to her spiritual health. "It would have been difficult to separate while we were getting over emotional attachments," she admits. "I would still have been praying for him, and we could have had some phone contact, but the romance would have had to end. I just could not get too serious with a non-Christian."

As with all aspects of your ministry to nonbelievers, your decisions must be based on common sense and the prompting of the Holy Spirit. That is why only believers who have strong relationships with God, and who have been called to evangelism through dating, should date nonbelievers. Most of us have *not* been called; to date nonbelievers, then, is to court disaster. So do yourself a favor. Unless your ministry lies here, be strong like an ox and resist the temptation to date nonbelievers. It'll keep you from being a donkey.

13.

Communication:
The Key to Intimacy

No one knows better how to make a friendship grow than the Lord. His words are the best guide for helping us achieve a loving and supportive relationship with another person. But *our* words, and what we say through our actions, are also important in relationships. In this chapter we want to share with you some tips for using effective communication to help your dating relationships grow.

One of the most important gifts God has given us is the ability to transfer meaning and understanding—by those grunts, groans, and strings of noises we call language, and by gestures and body movement. Communication between one another is essential to our physical and mental well-being; in fact, some scholars assert that without the ability to communicate people could not even survive.

But communication is much more than merely a survival tool! It is a vital element in maintaining relationships. If we did not have the ability to convey our feelings and opinions through words and deeds, no one would ever know we care for them. Adam and Eve communicated their love in the garden, and we've been using language and gestures to communicate love ever since.

How Communication Works—and Fails to Work

To better understand how we can use effective communication to help a relationship grow, let's take a few moments to talk about how we communicate with others—and why we sometimes fail to communicate what we really mean.

As we have indicated, communication has two parts—verbal and nonverbal. Verbal communication is made up of words, the

95

language of spoken symbols. Nonverbal communication con-
sists of gestures, tones of voice, body language, and other
means of conveying a message without actually speaking.
Nonverbal communication accounts for more than two-thirds
of the meaning we relay to one another.

Nonverbal communication often substitutes for spoken words.
When we catch a person's glance from across the room and
smile, we communicate, "I'm open," or "I'd like to meet you."
Conversely, through frowns, avoidance of eye contact, yawns,
or folded arms, we say we aren't open for conversation, that
we wish to be left alone.

Nonverbal communication also accents, clarifies, or even
contradicts what we say verbally. Consider the following
examples:

Joan and Barney are sitting on a park bench, not touching, but
with their bodies turned toward one another.

(1) Joan says, "But Barney, I love *you,*" putting the emphasis on
"you" while extending both arms, palms open, towards Barney.
(2) She says, "But Barney, I *love* you," in a squealy voice, drop-
ping her head and staring downward.
(3) She speaks the same phrase in a flat tone, keeping her arms
crossed in front of her and refusing to meet Barney's eyes.

Three very different meanings are conveyed here, although
the identical words, "I love you," are used. In the first example,
Joan may be trying to tell Barney she loves him and no one
else. In the second example, she may be pleading with him not
to break up their relationship, because she feels she cannot live
without him. In the third example, she may be the one who has
lost interest, although she can't yet bring herself to end the
relationship. The meaning, you see, is not totally in the spoken
words, but in the nonverbal messages that accompany the
words.

This is one reason communication can be so tricky—there's
more to it than just words. People can say one thing while
communicating something different nonverbally. And nonverbal signals can be misinterpreted; for instance, a failure to

make eye contact can be interpreted as a sign of insincerity when it actually indicates shyness or fear.

What makes communication even more challenging is that each of us is a very unique creation, with a different set of abilities, experiences, and attitudes. We bring these with us into the communication process, and they affect both what we say, verbally and nonverbally, and how we interpret what others say to us.

When you add up the factors that can sometimes hamper our ability to communicate, you can see why so many of us end up talking to each other without really understanding what the other is saying. Here are some simple principles for working against these communication problems:

(1) *Speak your thoughts clearly.* Don't be ambiguous and beat around the bush. Enunciate and speak forcefully.

(2) If you feel you aren't understood, *repeat important thoughts.*

(3) *Gain feedback* by asking questions like, "Do you understand?" or "Know what I mean?"

(4) *Check nonverbal feedback.* A smile, nod of the head, or utterance of a phrase like "Yeah" or "Hmmm" are good indications your message is being received. A frown or a wrinkled face may indicate confusion—and the need to repeat or clarify what you are saying.

Using Communication to Build Relationships

With these introductory thoughts in mind, let's explore five ways we can use verbal and nonverbal communication to achieve more intimacy—that special quality of closeness and caring—in our friendships and dating relationships:

(1) *Strive for transparency and self-disclosure.* The trust and love necessary to build intimacy in a relationship can only grow when the people involved risk revealing themselves as they really are—thoughts, feelings, and needs. In a relationship characterized by transparency, each partner assumes an attitude of "helper" and "confidant" for the other. Grant Howard writes about this kind of communication as he experiences it in his marriage:

Letting [my wife] in on my inner thoughts and feelings...
draws us closer together. Allowing her to ask questions, make
suggestions and even suffer together with me, deepens the intimacy of our relationship. The act of communication has tremen-
dous potential. When the truth is shared, the participants grow
up and together. That which edifies—unifies.[1]

In our discussions with single people, three questions about
self-disclosure in communication frequently come up. The first
question is, "Does self-disclosure mean telling everything—all
the time?" We believe the answer is "no." Although self-
disclosure is vitally important to building relationships, there
are times when "telling all" is not the best policy. Relationships differ; "it is unreasonable to attempt full disclosure with
everyone, or even with anyone at one sitting," notes Alan
McGinnis.[2] In the lives of most of us there are ghosts from the
past that are best left buried. These mistakes have been forgiven by God, and dredging them up will usually not do much
to help the relationship.

Having said this, we want to add that there are other times
when a "full disclosure" might be unifying. Janet Fix, author of
For Singles Only, began dating David Saint Pierre while com-
pleting the writing of that book. One day, while trying to sort
out what to include in the manuscript, she told David some of
the details of her past—including many things she had not told
even her best friends. Touched by her trust, David told his own
tale of overcoming a bondage to drugs. This act of mutual self-
disclosure drew them closer together as friends. They were
married less than a year later.

How can we determine when self-disclosure is appropriate?
First, by praying. James tells us, "If you want to know what
God wants you to do, ask him, and he will gladly tell you..."
(1:5, TLB). A prayer for wisdom can mean the difference between appropriate and inappropriate self-disclosure.

Second, use common sense. Some helpful advice is offered by
Adler and Towne, who say:

Telling life histories may make some people feel closer temporarily. But a growing relationship is built on the feelings and
reactions of events shared by those involved in the relationship.

Disclosing myself only through tales of my past history may help my partner know little more than the "me" of the past. You grow in a relationship when you learn how the other person feels about and reacts to what's going on between you in the present.

Appropriate self-disclosure is sharing how you are feeling about or reacting now to what's going on, or giving information about the past that's connected with your present feelings or reactions. We're not suggesting you openly share all yourself with everyone you know. This is neither possible nor practical. Openness comes from trust, and this takes some time to develop. But relationships do have to start somewhere, and experience shows that most people have stronger ones when they share more of themselves from the start.[3]

The second question we are often asked is, "Do I tell my friend only those things which will flatter him or her? Or can I criticize, too?" We certainly believe in telling others things that will flatter them! But constructive criticism can also help growth. When those who love us point out faults or weaknesses, they give us a chance to view ourselves from a different perspective—outside our own self-perceptions. If we really trust the judgments of those close to us, we will listen and consider what they say. In the same way, if we love those close to us, we will communicate with them about faults and weaknesses we think they possess.

Of course, constructive criticism must always be given in the context of love, and forgiveness should follow any discussion of another's weaknesses. The purpose of transparency and self-disclosure in communicating is building up the other person and the relationship—not tearing down the other person. We'll have much more to say about this in our next chapter.

A third question often asked is, "Should I tell only those things that put me in a good light?" No—telling only the good things defeats the purpose of self-disclosure. You'll recall that Janet and David told each other things which put them in a bad light. Yet their sharing led to intimacy in their relationship. Self-disclosure is not easy; it involves risk. When we reveal negative things about ourselves, we may get rejected or ridiculed. It may hurt to admit something from the past, even though that admission helps us illuminate present behavior.

What you choose to tell must be based on prayerful consideration and common sense. But self-disclosure is worth the risk.
McGinnis notes:

> In ways we do not fully understand, self-disclosure helps us to
> see things, feel things, imagine things, hope for things that we
> could never have thought possible. The invitation to transpa-
> rency, then, is really an invitation to authenticity.[4]

It's easy to talk about striving towards transparency. It's
quite another task to put the ideal into practice. The next four
suggestions for achieving intimacy through communication
will, we hope, give you some practical help as you begin to grow
in your relationship.

(2) *Communicate your feelings*. When we communicate with
others, there are three types of information we can convey—
facts, opinions, or feelings. At the beginning of a relationship,
we tend to reveal mainly facts about ourselves—our jobs,
where we live, our hobbies, our general likes and dislikes.
Then, as the relationship grows, we begin communicating information about our basic opinions and beliefs. This includes
political veiwpoints, theological backgrounds, our views on
dating, and some of our needs and feelings. But it is usually
only in deeper friendships that most of us feel free to express
what we feel inside. Feeling accepted, feeling we are in an
environment of trust, we tell each other our most secret
dreams, joys, and frustrations.

To truly communicate our feelings with each other, however,
even in intimate relationships, many of us have to unlearn
some cultural teaching. In chapter 4 we mentioned that, because of childhood conditioning, many men have difficulty expressing their feelings of tenderness, sorrow, or joy. Many are
ashamed of tears and suppress them, although, as McGinnis
says,

> Tears are a great gift from God—a safety valve built into our
> system—and there is no reason for us to be ashamed when they
> flow freely. We honor the other person when we cry. Our tears
> can start forth at moments of great joy, in the presence of beauty,
> or at times of sudden relief.[5]

It may not be easy, men, but honestly communicating emotions is an important part of growing towards intimacy. Work at learning to let the walls down. Women are often more open about expressing their feelings. They'd appreciate your doing the same.

Cherie's Comments:
Here's a good example of how detrimental male suppression of feelings can be. After dating John several times, I noticed that I felt lonely even after he left. I realized that I didn't know much about him—only where he worked and some superficial things about what he did in his spare time. I felt lonely because he really wasn't telling me much about himself.

So on our next date I told him that I really didn't know who he was or what he thought. I told him that deep down inside I knew he was a good person, but he was hiding behind self-erected walls. "You're burying yourself, and I don't know why" I said.

His response? He laughed. I asked him why he was laughing, because his response hurt me. He said my question was "very interesting."

I decided, for the moment, to let the subject drop. On our next date I was sure he had missed the point of everything I said. He never stopped talking and asking questions the whole time we were together—I almost choked on dinner trying to keep up with him. But still, he didn't tell me much about what he was feeling. We continued to discuss facts and opinions. And I continued to feel frustrated with the relationship!

Of course, men are not the only ones who have difficulty sharing their feelings. There are women who also find it difficult to cry and show tender feelings. And many women find it extremely difficult to express "negative" emotions such as anger. They have been taught the cultural stereotype that showing anger or confronting someone is not ladylike. "I was taught to be a nice little girl—not to show anger under any circumstances," Cherie recalls. "Showing anger was a real no-no, especially for a Christian girl."

Such passivity, however, can be a stumbling block to intimacy in relationships. We'll talk more about anger and how to express it appropriately in the next chapter, but, for the moment, suffice it to say that the true communication of feelings means expressing anger and criticism as well as tenderness and joy. If negative emotions are not expressed, they may remain stifled until they explode one day in a moment of frustration. By then it may be too late to mend the friendship.

(3) *Be liberal with praise.* A third way to help relationships grow through communication is to give compliments. People thrive on praise because it is a verbal reminder that they are loved and appreciated. Compliments tell us that our friends are tuning us in, noticing us, being sensitive to us. "The deepest principle in nature is the craving to be appreciated," psychologist William James has noted.[6] Many a friendship has stagnated because the friends stopped complimenting each other.

It is usually not hard to find things you can compliment your friends on. "If you train your mind to search for the positive things about other people, you will be surprised at how many good things you can observe in them and comment upon," McGinnis notes.[7] Be especially liberal with praise when your friend or date seems to be having a bad day. And compliment the unexpected—not just the way he or she looks or dresses. Try praising a person's sense of humor, singing voice, kindness, or other good qualities. Use your creativity in finding ways to express the compliment! You might send flowers, along with a simple note that says, "Thanks for being my friend." Or you might write a thank-you card, or buy a gift (a toy model of his favorite car, a miniature bottle of perfume) that shows you think your friend is a special person.

One final note on praise. Praise, like love, is to be freely given. Don't pay compliments in hopes of receiving them in return. Freely give and you shall freely receive out of the sincerity of others' hearts.

(4) *Listen.* Another way to grow closer to your friendship is to listen—really listen—to each other. "The greatest compliment a man ever paid me," Thoreau once wrote, "was when he asked me a question and then listened to my answer."

By listening we do several things. First, we gain insight into the personality, experiences, and needs of our friends. We become more sensitive, better able to help them. In addition, when we provide them with feedback on what they say, we help them better understand themselves.

"Active listening" is the term used to describe this process of
carefully listening, then repeating back to the speaker what
you understood him or her to have said. For instance, Kenny
may tell Cherie he was really frustrated trying to write a chapter of this book. Cherie, actively listening, might then respond
by asking, "It really challenged you, did it? How?" By listening
to Kenny's statement, and responding to it, Cherie may help
him better explore his feelings or behavior. Another good tech-
nique of active listening is to repeat the other person's last
statement to them, beginning with, "What I heard you saying
was. . . . "

We can increase our effectiveness as listeners by using nonverbal responses to show the speaker we're listening. To show
that you're interested in what your friend is saying, tilt your
body slightly toward him or her, and maintain eye contact.
Don't let your wandering eyes tell that you aren't completely
tuned in, and don't show defensiveness by crossing your arms
across your chest. Use facial expressions to respond to what
you're hearing: try a smile, a grimace, a nod of the head—
whatever is appropriate.

A good listener is a good friend. That's the way God planned
it to be. Notes philosopher Zeno of Citium, "We have been
given two ears and but a single mouth, in order that we may
hear more and talk less.

(5) *Coming Before the Lord*—A final way to grow in a friendship through communication is to communicate with the
Lord—to actively submit that relationship to Christ. He is the
source of all fulfillment, and the source of strength for your
dating relationships. To submit your relationship to the Lord,
you and your date need to make a commitment to times of
worship, prayer, and Bible study together. While it might be
impractical to spend all of your time together in prayer and
study, we've found that couples who pray together either at the
beginning or close of their dates feel they have a smoother time
with one another. When Jesus is an active participant in the
dating relationship, there can't help but be more honesty and
openness. And that means growth.

If you begin to put these five ideas into practice, you'll find
your friendships becoming more enjoyable and more intimate.
Of course, you'll still have some difficult and frustrating

times—we're all human. So we counsel patience. It takes time to mold a deep friendship, and the road might sometimes get rocky. Also, the Lord's timing is not always our own, and his purposes might be different from ours. So be patient and allow God to work his will in your friendship—to nurture it at his chosen speed. If you run ahead of him, or try to mold the relationship into something he does not want it to be—you'll be frustrated indeed.

Even with a patient spirit, though, there will be times when our friendships and dating relationships run into confrontations. And that isn't always bad!

14.

Confrontation: An Ally of Intimacy

Kenny's Comment:
   There hadn't been any open disagreements, but I had this sense that something was amiss. Call it vibrations, maybe. I knew that when I had left Diane's house the last two times I had felt unfulfilled and somehow frustrated.
   She wanted our friendship to be platonic; she felt the need to sort through some of her attitudes without the responsibility of a romantic relationship. In my heart I knew I wanted a romantic relationship. I had hugged that idea as I hugged her. But I thought I had been fairly cool about the relationship and just concentrating on having fun. Was she feeling pressure from me anyway and responding by pulling back?
   Or was it something else?
   For my peace of mind, I needed answers. How would I get them?
   Obviously, I could ask.
   But what if my fears were confirmed and she wanted to stop seeing me? Wouldn't it be better to wait and let the situation take care of itself? Maybe the vibrations would just go away. But I knew that such situations rarely take care of themselves.
   What if we got mad at each other and quarreled?
   What if I was just imagining things and nothing was wrong?
   Well, I worried about it for a few days, not eating very well. I decided at first just not to talk to her for a week in hope that all negative feelings would go away. But that decision increased my frustration. We'd had a straightforward, honest relationship. Hadn't we said we were dedicated to friendship, and that friends talk openly about things that bother them? That's the path to growth. By not confronting the situation I was being

selfish, putting my insecurities in the way of an opportunity for better understanding. Certainly an open airing of differences would also be in Diane's best interest.

Finally I called, and we talked for a few minutes. The conversation seemed slow, and confirmed my feeling that something was wrong. With some hesitation, I commented that a remark she had made a few days before had bothered me. She countered by saying she felt the need to talk about where we were going in our relationship.

We decided to get together immediately. A few minutes later we were seated in a quiet corner of a local ice cream parlor. As we talked, Diane confirmed that she felt I had handled a particular situation poorly, and also that she was feeling pressure not only from me, but also from her friends who wanted us to "get together." We talked through these feelings in an open, nonjudgmental manner, and we discovered that both of us had let others' expectations sidetrack us from what we really wanted for our friendship. We reconfirmed our desire to concentrate on a platonic friendship since both of us had tendencies to "fall in love" with love rather than with people. By concentrating on friendship, we felt we would be better able to share ourselves with each other without trying to "win" each other's affection.

We ended the night in prayer. Both of us felt much better, like a load had been lifted from our spirits.

As I drove home that night I thought about other heart-to-heart talks I had had with women. Some had resulted in the end of our relationship; my feelings that something was wrong had been confirmed and we had broken up. But far more often the interchange had led to a deepening of our friendship. I had learned some valuable things about myself and often felt affirmed as a person of worth and merit.

Confrontation is not always easy, but it is usually worth the effort. Time and time again, God has confirmed that to me. Slowly I'm learning, and it feels good.

It's true that some of our most difficult conversations can be catalysts for growth. When we disagree with another and honestly communicate about that disagreement, we often grow closer. In the quest for intimacy in relationships, confrontation is our greatest ally. Muriel James and Louis Savaray note:

Friendships without differences are sometimes more limiting than freeing. Honest disagreements can be exciting and creative when they are not used as putdowns but are designed to open further avenues of thought.[1]

Most of us have probably been in a few discussions that weren't conducive to growth. Maybe one partner felt he or she had to "win" the discussion. Unless both people enter a discussion with a conciliatory, loving attitude, it is difficult to reach understanding. A friendship can be severely damaged.

The Christian attitude toward confrontations and disagreements is expressed in the Beatitude, "Blessed are the peacemakers, for they shall be called sons of God" (Matt. 5:9, NAS). Paul adds that love is "patient and kind" (1 Cor. 13:4, RSV). This principle of working towards loving, peaceful confrontations applies even in situations where we are convinced we are right. As you may recall, Jesus told those who would criticize others to "first take the log out of your own eye..." (Matt. 7:1-5, RSV) a caution that each of us needs to confront our own shortcomings when we talk with another about his or her problem areas.

The type of relationship that best handles occasional confrontations is profiled by James and Savaray, who say that in these relationships:

(1) Friends share a deep commitment to work things through.

(2) They know communication skills for dealing with stress.

(3) They tend to be flexible and tolerant of each other's idiosyncracies;

(4) They expect important relationships to have some stress.

(5) They are basically optimistic about their relationship.[2]

To help you learn the communication skills necessary for "dealing with stress" we've compiled thirteen tips for successful confrontation. If you take heed of these, your encounters will be more productive and growth-producing:

(1) When a situation that "bugs" you arises, or you have a feeling something is amiss, *get a handle on your emotions.* Don't speak out quickly, in the heat of emotion. Think through what is bothering you. Write it down, if necessary, to clarify it in your own mind.

(2) *Pray for God's direction and wisdom.* Ask him to help you see the situation accurately, and to express love as you talk.

(3) *Be sensitive to timing.* There are good times and bad times to introduce a problem. If either of you is not in the proper frame of mind, postpone your heart-to-heart talk. If it seems that talking is absolutely necessary, then proceed prayerfully.

(4) *Try to talk where you can meet face-to-face.* Seek a comfortable and private spot. Allow adequate time for discussion and prayer.

(5) *Cultivate a positive outlook.* Such discussions usually mean change for both you and your date. But change can be for the better: it can draw you closer together, and it can help you learn more about yourself. So be positive about the encounter.

(6) *Be specific about introducing your concern.* What single action or attitude bothers you? State it clearly.

(7) *Present your concern in "I" language.* Tell your friend how his or her actions make *you* feel. Don't condemn them for what they did.

For instance, you might begin a conversation by saying, "When you smoke cigarettes, it makes me feel . . ." In a confrontation of this type, always talk about how you feel rather than attacking the other person.

(8) *Ask; don't assume.* A certain tentativeness should be evident in your statements. What you think is happening may not be what your friend thinks is happening. So don't present an interpretation of his or her behavior as fact. Rather, say, "I gather from what you're saying that. . . . Am I right?" Or, "It seems to me that. . . . Right?"

(9) *Offer suggestions* for change you'd like to see.

(10) *Seek feedback* to make sure the other person understands what you are saying.

(11) *Forget past problems.* Concern yourself only with the present issue.

(12) *Raise only one issue at a time.* Don't confuse the situation by bringing up other problems. If a number of issues need discussing, then take them one at a time.

(13) *Be willing to compromise* out of love. Mark Knapp, author of *Social Intercourse* writes,

Compromise is the hallmark of constructive conflict and more often than not, the ability to compromise arises out of the ability to understand that our partner's view of reality is just as real and just as right as ours.[3]

The only time you should not compromise is when there is absolutely no doubt in your mind that God is speaking through you to correct another's behavior.

There is one caution to these words on constructive conflict. They reflect the thinking of humans. Therefore they should be considered as guidelines only. If the Lord lays another course of action on your heart, follow it. Sometimes a direct confrontation, in which you are used of the Lord to reprove someone, is called for. Sometimes a letter, thoughtfully and lovingly written out, is a better way to bring a concern to the attention of a friend. We only suggest that you approach such a situation with much prayer and common sense.

These tips aren't all-inclusive, either. We've left out some concerns we're sure you would like answered:

What happens when I do get angry and explode at my friend?

Because none of us is perfect, there will be times when we do get angry. What we need to do is channel that outburst into a constructive channel. Paul tells us not to let the sun go down on our anger; these are wise words when we have just exploded at someone (see Eph. 4:26,27). So when there has been an angry outburst, by all means first regain your composure. Then sit down with your friend and calmly discuss whatever led to the outburst. We suggest you begin the session by apologizing for letting your own emotions get out of control. That will set a conciliatory foundation for your discussion.

I want to confront people but it is difficult because I'm shy. What can I do?

You might begin the conversation by saying, "I feel really uncomfortable about discussing this, but..." Or you might substitute *fearful, scared,* or *anxious* for *uncomfortable.* You might begin by asking, "May I tell you something that is bothering me?" With this introduction, you will usually gain a sympathetic ear. Your friend will listen less defensively because you began with this humble approach.

Shouldn't men be the ones initiating confrontations?

Either sex can initiate a confrontation. In fact, because of cultural hang-ups, many men find it difficult to confront. Carole Altman, a psychologist, has suggested that women may be uniquely trained to initiate confrontations. She says men have been trained to be competitive, and are often oriented towards the "win/lose" confrontation. This has paralyzed them emotionally when it comes to confrontations between friends. "In our society *most* men are trained *out* of abilities such as being less competitive, being sensitive, being able to empathize, to listen to others, or to show their feelings," she says. She later adds, "I suggest that relationships can and do work—if women wake up to their *responsibilities*.... I suggest that females take more initiative to help the male with tasks which are difficult—or impossible—for him."[4] The woman might help the man, then, by saying "What's the matter?" or "I feel a strain in our relationship" or "You seem angry about something. Would you like to talk about it?"

How should I respond when a friend confronts me?

Listen. You will learn something valuable about yourself that you didn't know before. What better way for God to speak to us than through a loved and trusted friend? "To be criticized is often to be truly appreciated," Augsburger says, "to be respected so much that the other person can share both his positive and negative feelings with you. To be criticized by a real friend is to be loved."[5] When someone confronts you, hear them out. Then prayerfully evaluate what they have said. God's spirit will reveal to you the truth or error of what you have been told.

But sometimes they may ask me to make changes I just can't make.

Why not? You can change old patterns of behavior if you want to. Augsburger says:

Can people change? Can life be new? Can life be different? Wrong questions. Wrong words. Wrong viewpoints. It's not "can we" but "will we." Strength is available. Change is possible. Whenever a man or a woman accepts responsibility for where he is (that's often called confession) and chooses to make a change (that's often called repentance) and reaches out for the strength of God and the acceptive love of some significant other persons (that's called conversion) then change begins.[6]

What if I want to break up?

Then do it. Breaking up is very difficult to do, and we don't want to minimize the trauma of telling someone you don't want to see them much any more. But it is more advantageous to both you and your friend if you end a relationship that is no longer growing rather than having it drag on.

Whenever you are breaking up, do so with humility and love. Be as positive about the other person as you can. Compliment what you have enjoyed about being with them. Then state specifically that you would like to end the relationship and, if possible, explain why. Remember, it is helpful if you dwell on your feelings rather than criticizing another's personality or actions. It is better to say, "The last few times we've been together I've felt unfulfilled because I really think we have different goals for our relationship, and different goals in life." This is much more affirming than saying, "I don't like being with you any more because you're boring."

After you've broken up, you may be tempted to try to get together again when you are lonely, "just to see how you're doing." But, if you have really hurt someone by breaking up, give them some recovery time before you try to revive a casual friendship. And, by all means, if you feel strongly about breaking up, then stick to your resolve. Don't let the other person talk you into continuing if your heart is set on ending something that is not producing growth and happiness.

After we've had our heart-to-heart talk, how should it end?

Whether your talk resulted in closer growth or a break-up, try to end by taking the situation to the Lord.

Cherie's Comments:

I once had a man tell me he wanted to stop seeing me because I was "boring." Needless to say, I was devastated. But had this man been a Christian who would have prayed with me after that revelation and been willing to work with me in friendship, I know I would have progressed much faster towards becoming a more interesting and self-confident person. I really believe that confrontation should be followed by prayer, because I believe that God's will in confronting another person is to also build them up.

It is also healing to follow up a confrontation with another conversation a few days later. Use that time to report on progress of actions and feelings. Encourage one another. Pray together for continued growth.

Achieving true intimacy in friendship requires open and positive attitudes about confrontation. There are times, of course, when a confrontation will end a friendship and you will be the one being rejected. Growth can occur even then.

15.

Surviving a Break-Up

No one likes to break up. Yet it happens all the time. When someone breaks up with us, we go through all sorts of emotions. Sometimes we may lean on God for help; sometimes we may blame him for causing our hurt and look for solace in the world's answers. In this chapter we want to offer solace for those who are struggling with a broken relationship. We've been through enough of them to know that each circumstance is different. What works for one person may not necessarily work for another. But what remains constant is God's desire to heal our hurts, to help us through the difficult times, to help us risk and love again.

It's a fact of life that relationships end. Usually one of us wants to keep dating, or stay married, while the other wants to call it quits. Someone usually ends up feeling like the break-up is the end of the world. Pain, fear of the future, loneliness—all beset us. Sometimes we might even feel we are going crazy. But rest assured that such feelings are normal. Author Toby Hempel notes:

> To feel sorry at the end of a relationship indicates that you are a person capable of deep emotions, a person who recognizes the importance of commitment and who possesses a serious character, devoid of superficiality and shallowness. To feel sorry is to be human.[1]

While feeling sorry is a human response, so is the desire to be healed of the pain. We all desire to move through the breaking-up period to the enjoyment of new dating relationships.

In this process the Christian who hurts has a great advan-

tage over the hurting non-Christian. God has promised his
people he will never leave them. His love and desire to help us
is assured; we need only ask. Jesus says:

> "Come to me all of you who are weary and over-burdened, and I
> will give you rest! Put on my yoke and learn from me. For I am
> gentle and humble in heart and you will find rest for your souls.
> For my yoke is easy and my burden is light" (Matt. 11:28–30,
> Phillips).

In our fast-paced world, where major crises are resolved on
television in thirty minutes, God's timetable for healing may
seem slow. But his ways are sure. He knows what he is doing,
and what he's doing will ultimately work for your good. Pastor
Billy Dobrenen, of Calvary Chapel in Costa Mesa, California,
notes, "The best things come hard. While our society is at-
tempting to avoid all pain and discomfort at any cost, God has
revealed in His Word that suffering and hard times can have
glorious effects on our lives."[2] And the Apostle Paul assures us:
"Moreover we know that to those who love God, who are called
according to his plan, everything that happens fits into a pattern for good" (Rom. 8:28, Phillips).

Clearly, God's love is our ally. When we hurt, we need to
turn to him for help. Turning elsewhere—to singles' bars, old
flames, non-Christian friends, or depression—will only sidetrack the healing you desire.

Pat Chavez, author of *Picking Up the Pieces,* is twice divorced. Pat jumped into her second marriage rather hastily.
After it broke up, she almost remarried her first husband. But
as her hopes were soaring, he coldly informed her that he had
decided to marry someone else. Traumatized, living with a ter-
rible self-image and feeling like she was going crazy, Pat
turned to the Lord. In him she found hope and—most
important—she found love. Pat writes:

> Until you feel loved . . . genuinely, deeply loved, you're going to
> feel inferior. Insecure. Fragile. And you're probably going to lash
> out at others—just to protect yourself.
> But I said there was hope. And I meant it. When everywhere I
> turned my world was loveless and everything inside me cried out
> that I didn't deserve to be loved, help came from an unexpected

Resource, one I didn't even know was there. Quietly, yet very clearly, God let me see that He loved me . . . just as I was. Somehow He broke through my pain and mental panic to help me know that He understood what I was feeling and hadn't rejected me.

Please don't dismiss this as glib, pious God-talk. Out of my own experience I could not offer you any more realistic, more concrete, more genuinely helpful advice.

Go to God. Pour out your pain and your anger. As simply, as directly as you can, tell Him what you are feeling. Let it all out. He won't be surprised or shocked. Then, as the anger subsides, allow Him to let you know how much He loves you, and how much He wants to love you into a complete recovery from this difficult experience.[3]

A second great healer of hurt is Father Time. Social scientists tell us it may take a year or two to fully recover from the death of a spouse or a divorce. If you are recovering from a serious dating relationship, it may take months before you are ready to begin dating again.

Time is also the great equalizer of those erratic mood shifts most people experience after a break-up. Whenever you are hurting, take a few minutes and look at the long-range workings of God in your life. Think about where you were five years ago, and about how much God has done for you since then. Comfort yourself by looking at how God worked through difficult circumstances in the past. Also, remind yourself that his timetable for our lives is different from ours. He requires of us that we have faith—sometimes the kind of faith that grits its teeth and says, "I will stand firm and believe, even though I don't see anything good happening." Rest assured, our Father's perfect love for us means that something is happening, even if we can't see it.

As you trust God and time to heal the pain of a break-up, you might want to consider the following suggestions for helping you get back on your feet again:

(1) When your partner says it's **over**, *don't try to change his or her mind.* Maybe it is *not* God's will that you break up. Maybe your partner *is* acting outside of God's plan. But, for the moment, accept what has been said. Arguing with someone who has made up his or her mind will be fruitless. Then, if your

friend doesn't suggest that the two of you pray together, ask for the time. It is hard to pray with someone who has hurt you. But if you are able to take this very painful moment before God, he can begin the healing process that much more quickly. Also, when two people come before the Lord with differences, it is much more difficult for them to part in bitterness or hatred. The Holy Spirit will act as a healing agent between you, whether or not you remain active friends.

(2) *Accept the end of the relationship.* Often we cling to a hope that our "ex" will come to his or her senses and ask us back. Usually that hope is unreal. Sure, we've heard stories in which one person suddenly "woke up" and begged the other to take him or her back. And, so the story goes, they lived happily ever after. But the odds of this happening to you are slim. So, difficult as letting go may be, you must begin to accept the end of the relationship. If God intends for you to get back together again, you will—with or without your striving and scheming. Your task is to surrender all your earthly desires to God so he can have permission from your spirit to begin a healing work within you. As Peter tells us: "And after you have suffered for a little, the God of all grace, who called you to His eternal glory in Christ, will Himself perfect, confirm, strengthen and establish you" (1 Pet. 5:10, NAS).

Often we have trouble "letting go" because we fear the future. We want to cling to the old and familiar patterns of having a sure date, a close companion, a trusted friend. We want to cling to memories, no matter how painful they may be now, because they are familiar. They are "better" than the uncertainty of "getting back into circulation."

It *is* true that reentering the dating scene again can be traumatic; many people report feeling as if they were fifteen years old again—playing games and feeling insecure. But we must do it! We must let go of the past and look to the future. There's an old, anonymous, and very profound statement that says:

> Turn somebody loose.
> If they return, they are yours;
> If they don't, they never were.

That's sound advice.

(3) *Forgive you "ex" for any pain he or she has caused you,* or bitterness will soon rear its ugly head. Forgiveness is a process, and it will take time. Pat Chavez notes:

> You must come to the realization within your own heart that to forgive someone else is something God wants you to do for *yourself* more than for the other person. Not to forgive means eventually to make yourself mentally, emotionally, and physically ill. It's always possible to forgive.... I'm not saying you can do it without God's grace, but you can do it.[4]

The Apostle Paul says:

> And do not grieve the Holy Spirit of God, by whom you were sealed for the day of redemption. Let all bitterness and wrath and anger and clamor and slander be put away from you, along with all malice. And be kind to one another, tender-hearted, forgiving each other, just as God in Christ also has forgiven you. (Eph. 4:30–32, NAS).

(4) *Don't bounce into another relationship.* When we are "on the rebound," we're emotionally susceptible to all kinds of temptations. The temptation to seek solace in the arms of another will be strong. Instead, seek comfort from close friends who will have your best interests at heart. Lean on the Lord for love and understanding, rather than rushing off to another relationship.

(5) *Don't turn down invitations for social occasions.* Get into circulation again; stay busy.

(6) *Put some physical distance between you and the other person.* If you had a favorite park, restaurant, or other place, stay away from it for a while. Also, take all physical reminders—photos, special gifts, clothing you wore only for him or her—and put them in storage for a while. Let the memories settle until you get back on an even emotional keel.

(7) *Keep a notebook.* Record your daily thoughts as you work through the process of grief and healing. Vent your feelings on paper. And, as time progresses, see how God is working to heal

you as your pain subsides and you begin to have hope for new friendships.

(8) *Seek physical comfort.* One aspect of breaking up is losing physical affection from your date. Wanderer and Cabot suggest you compensate for this loss by seeking some physical comfort from friends: "Try increasing the amount of physical affection you give and receive each day," they say. "Make your first goal at least one hug this week. Each week increase by one hug, until you are getting at least four warm, cuddly, bear-like squeezes weekly."[5]

(9) During the first few weeks of recovery, you may need to *interrupt thoughts of the past.* To dwell on what was or what could be—to think of past times together—may lead to depression or self-pity. Toby Hempel notes:

> To break a habit, you must identify it first, and cut it off abruptly whenever it makes an appearance. Therefore, to break the habit of thinking constantly about your lover you must deflect and interrupt the essentially counterproductive thought processes that have gotten underway. These are responsible for impeding your progress.[6]

Hempel suggests that if you get these thoughts while alone, you can derail them by clapping loudly, banging on a table, or yelling "no." "Anything abrupt, violent, loud and shocking is extremely effective in cutting off the unproductive thought," she says.[7]

The Goal

Whenever adversity strikes, the ultimate goal for the Christian is to arrive on the other side with a stronger relationship with Christ. To be able to say, "Thank you, Lord, for those circumstances, and for what I learned through them" is the essence of growth.

Another goal we hope you achieve is to maintain a friendship with the person who hurt you. We realize that this is not always possible. But when you've invested much time and love in someone, it's a shame to be completely cut off from his or her friendship just because the romance has died. We can testify to the value of working to "stay friends." Each of us has cultivated some close friendships with people we used to date. In fact, when our friendship began, we dated romantically, but most of this book has been written after the romantic feelings stopped. We're best friends now, and we highly recommend the extra effort it takes to forge such a friendship.

Risking Again

Having been hurt in a dating relationship, many of us find ourselves reluctant to take risks again. We want to insulate our feelings from further shock by not taking chances on getting hurt. This is natural, and probably necessary. In fact, for a while we do suggest that you treat yourself with kid gloves. Don't be anxious to rush into relationships that might do further damage to your self-image.

But eventually you must step out again and take the risk of developing other relationships. Withdrawing into a cocoon gets you no closer to your goal of getting married or of enjoying meaningful friendships with members of the opposite sex. And there's another reason it is important to take the risk of reaching out, even after you have been hurt:

> Risk must be taken, because the greatest hazard in life is to risk nothing. The person who risks nothing does nothing, has nothing and is nothing. He may avoid suffering and sorrow, but he simply cannot learn, grow, feel, change, love, live. Chained by his certitudes, he is a slave, he has forfeited freedom. Only a person who risks is free.[8]

We have said a lot in this chapter about how to live through a break-up. But that may not be an issue for you at the moment. Your "special" dating relationship may be going perfectly—so perfectly, in fact, that you are feeling intense physical desires. Those desires are natural, of course, but how they are expressed is of prime concern to the Lord. He has his own ideas about human sexuality and sexual expression between man and woman. And why shouldn't he? He was the one who created sexuality!

16.

Sex

We read throughout the Bible that human sexuality is a gift from God. He made us male and female for a purpose. We can't exist without each other. Obviously, the human race has no other way to reproduce. But, more importantly, we need each other for encouragement, personal communication, and sharing love and intimacy. According to biblical teaching, we are meant to enjoy the ultimate expression of our sexuality—intercourse—as a part of a "need/giving" relationship with another. The fusion of two people through sexual intercourse is symbolic of the emotional and spiritual unity that comes when two people commit themselves to each other and to God. "Sex does not make love," notes Jerry Evans. "At its best, it expresses love."[1]

Since God made sexuality and its expression through intercourse, we know that he also gave us erotic passion and the ability to experience physical ecstacy. Notice in Genesis 2:24 that God created a man and a woman, brought them together in marriage, and then told them to "become one flesh." They became "one flesh" by having sexual intercourse. We are also told earlier that God looked down on his creation and saw that it was good (Gen. 1:31). Sexual intercourse and sexual passion were created before the fall of man—and therefore they are part of God's perfect plan for us. Lewis B. Smedes, in *Sex for Christians*, writes:

> God did not wince when Adam, in seeing Eve, was moved to get close to her. Male and female were created sexual to be sexual together. When Adam and Eve . . . clung together in the soft grass of Eden, wild with erotic passion, and were finally fulfilled in their love, we may suppose that God looked on and smiled. It

could not have entered God's mind that when His two creatures were sexually aroused, they were submitting to a demonic lust percolating up from some subhuman abyss to ensnare their virgin souls.[2]

That sexual union is meant to be a beautiful experience is evident from even a cursory reading of the Song of Solomon, or Proverbs 5:18, 19, which says:

> Let your fountain be blessed,
> And rejoice in the wife of your youth.
> As a loving hind and a graceful doe,
> Let her breasts satisfy you at all times;
> Be exhilarated always with her love (NAS).

Since our Father has created and pronounced his blessing on sexual expression, you would expect to find an attitude of "the joy of sex" permeating our churches. But sex has become the church's only three-letter "four-letter word." In the past, and even today, Christians—fearing sexual sins like fornication, adultery, and homosexuality—have taught that *all* sex is dirty, that it is a necessary evil for procreation, that it is something women have to endure for the sake of fulfilling the "animal" lusts of the male. Some people are so hung up on the fear of sex that they blanch every time the word is uttered in public. They just can't believe something so "earthy" is a part of God's great spiritual scheme for man. Bert H. Hodges notes:

> In the Christian order of things, bodies are to be denied, covered up, and kept in the background. Ultimately we hope to overcome our bodies or escape them; then we will be like Christ, we think. In this view bodily pleasure is especially suspect, as revealed in that bit of folklore we so carelessly repeat, "If it feels good, it must be a sin."[3]

Secular society, of course, has in recent years taken the opposite approach to sexuality. For many people the dictum is, "If it feels good, do it"—with whomever and in whatever circumstances you choose. Instead of seeing intercourse as a mysterious, God-ordained unification of husband and wife, they describe it as a simple biological function. Many men we've talked to take it for granted that a woman will go to bed with them on the first date. They expect sex as a reward for taking the woman out and showing her a good time.

The irony is that this same society which claims sex is just as natural and trivial as going to the bathroom or saying "thank you" seems at the same time to worship sexuality as a god. Sexiness is such a desired quality that sex is used effectively to sell jockey shorts, toothpaste, floor wax, and designer jeans. The creativity of Madison Avenue—finding sexual attractiveness in a freshly waxed floor—is unbelievable. But somehow they make us believe, "Using this product will increase your sex appeal."

The worship of sex in contemporary society has led many to place undue emphasis on physical attractiveness. A woman with long legs and a tan can become a goddess of our society— as evidenced by the accolades we heap on the sex queen of the moment. Even young people pick up on these warped standards. A high school teacher shared with us recently that freshman boys constantly harrass her with barbed comments about her sexuality. One boy was even so bold as to ask for her measurements right in front of the rest of the class. It is evident that many in our contemporary world worship the creature, rather than following the Creator's plan for sexual enjoyment.

Our society's warped and paradoxical views of sex are producing a variety of confused and warped actions. And the further our sexual mores drift from our Creator's plan, the more disillusioned and unfulfilled we become. But God's perfect plan has never changed. Sexual intimacy is God's special design for procreation, pleasure, and the intimate union of two people who are married. This is the only lifestyle that offers true fulfillment.

Sex and the Single Christian

How does all this relate to the single Christian? The Bible has some specific things to say about sex and singles, and its message is neither "sex is dirty" nor "sex is everything." According to God's Handbook, the act of sexual intercourse is a wonderful gift from God that is reserved *only* for two people who have made a lifetime commitment to one another. To violate God's plan—to engage in intercourse outside marriage—is sin. This sin is called either "fornication"—sexual intercourse between two single persons, or "adultery"—sexual relations involving two people, one or both of whom are married.

In the Old Testament, God often spoke out against sexual sin. He even included a commandment against it as one of his basic laws for the children of Israel (See Exod. 20:14). Also in the Old Testament, God occasionally compared fornication and adultery to idolatry; in Ezekial 16 we read that God used "harlotry"—fornication with a prostitute—as a metaphor for what the Jews had done in turning their backs on him to worship foreign gods.

The New Testament also makes it evident that God considers sex outside marriage a sin (see 1 Thess. 4:3, Eph. 5:3). In 1 Corinthians 6:17-20, Paul states that sexual sins are harmful to ourselves and offensive to God:

> But if you give yourself to the Lord, you and Christ are joined together as one person. That is why I say to run from sex sin. No other sin affects the body as this one does. When you sin this sin it is against your own body. Haven't you yet learned that your body is the home of the Holy Spirit God gave you, and that he lives within you? Your body does not belong to you. For God has bought you with a great price. So use every part of your body to give glory back to God, because he owns it (TLB).

God's Word is very clear on this subject, then: sexual intercourse outside marriage is sinful. Smedes tells us,

> Sexual intercourse does not unite two people forever in an absolute, literal sense, unless they intend to be united. . . . It is a sensual act with spiritual implications, a physical act with an inner meaning. Therefore the act is immoral unless it is joined by an intention to accept what the inner meaning signifies.[4]

Actually, there are some important psychological, as well as moral, reasons for following God's commands when it comes to sex outside of marriage. We have emphasized that Christian dating should be based on principles of friendship with those

we date; let's look at the physical expression of sexuality
within this context. Sex outside marriage can sidetrack us
from our goal of achieving an intimacy of sharing and giving
with another person. Physical desire is so strong that it can
dominate all other aspects of the relationship. "Sex inhibits the
development of a love relationship because as soon as we let it
on stage, it steals the entire show," notes Evans.[5] He also cor-
rectly states that sexual desire can lead to a pseudo-intimacy, a
counterfeit closeness. "When we want to be close to someone we
will use the easy route to intimacy: sex. The result is that we
neglect the other levels of closeness that usually take more
work. You do not learn to understand someone by "pouncing"
on him or her."[6]

Still another reason for controlling sexual expression in our
dating relationships is guilt. Most of us are aware of God's
teachings about sex. So when we do have sex outside marriage,
we feel guilty. We want to do what is right before God, yet we
are often tempted by—and many of us succumb to—the desire
for physical expression with another. Knowing that we have
sinned against God and our own bodies, and that we have par-
ticipated in sin with another, can have devastating
psychological—and even physical—effects.

Kenny's Comments:
   For weeks I suffered from nausea and shooting pains in my
stomach. I went through bottles of Pepto Bismol. I thought
maybe it was something I had eaten. Then I decided it was
abnormal stress from my master's degree program. I went to the
school doctor for tests, only to find there was no ulcer or infec-
tion. The doctor suggested a vacation.
   The pain continued. At about the same time, I decided that a
dating relationship was not going in the right direction. I found
my desires becoming more and more dominated by the thought
of being able to touch, kiss, and caress the woman I was dating.
In a sense we were flirting with suicide as we spent our time
together exploring each other's bodies. As a result, the spiritual
side of our relationship had all but disappeared. We went to
church still, but it was out of a sense of duty.
   Not knowing the real problem, my girlfriend and I decided to
stop seeing each other for awhile, because both of us agreed we

were "in a rut." Although I felt some emotional pain at our separation, I noticed at the same time that my stomach pains had ceased. We didn't get back together. And my stomach pains didn't return.

In retrospect, I believe that guilt was causing a physical reaction. I was involved in a relationship that was out of context with God's plan. I knew that, but kept on with the relationship because I liked the physical aspect. And my feelings of guilt, suppressed by my selfishness, finally took a physical toll on me.

You may believe that the psychological reasons for abstinence are not applicable to you. Perhaps you feel you invest an adequate amount of time and effort in getting to know someone before you decide to have sex. Perhaps you don't feel especially guilty about having intercourse. But that still does not exempt you from the spiritual reasons for not having sex.

There are physical laws that govern the way our bodies function. Violating these laws—for instance, not eating the proper foods or not getting enough sleep—will result in physical problems. In the same way, violating spiritual laws will guarantee eventual spiritual problems—although we may not be aware of these until much later.

Unanswered Questions

Some of you no doubt have problems dealing with God's directives about the expression of sexual intercourse. You aren't alone. A recent survey of divorced Christians at a large church showed that many in the church are not acting according to God's Handbook. Only nine percent of the men and twenty-seven percent of the women had been celibate since the end of their marriages. The rest of this group of "born again" believers were sexually active, some having had relations more than fifty times since their divorces. One-fourth of the men said celibacy was unrealistic, while half the women said it was not possible to practice.

The people were asked why they chose to be sexually active. One answered, "You don't turn off sexual desire like a water faucet." Another said, "We all have needs, and after thirty-two years of marriage, they can't be turned off all at once." In order of importance, the group listed loneliness, strong sex drive, "it is natural," reaffirmation of sexual attractiveness, fear, retaliation, "to dull the pain" of a break-up, and boredom as the main reasons for engaging in sexual intercourse.[7]

Let's take a closer look at some of these—and other reasons—for having sex outside of marriage:

(1) "*I'm so lonely.*" Loneliness is probably the biggest reason for engaging in sex outside of marriage. Singles bars are full of lonely people, all in search of fulfillment. Unfortunately, the environment of bars encourages one-night stands. And real needs aren't met by a romp in the sack. Smedes says:

> When one uses his genitals to escape the aloneness of his life, he is bound to be cast even deeper into the prison cell of loneliness.... The quick sexual encounter, repeated over and over, is not a gasp of hope but a private drama of hopelessness: "What the hell?" "Why not?" But the kernel of what sexuality could mean is still present, and the dim memory of it serves only to drive the actors more deeply into despair.[8]

By using sex as a cure for loneliness, we treat a symptom, not a cause. Real fulfillment comes from our relationship with God and the caring, supportive love of friends. To forsake this and seek a momentary end to loneliness through intercourse is counterproductive and can be damaging to our sense of self-worth.

(2) Another frequently heard comment is: "*If I don't go to bed with him, I'll lose him (her).*" This is another myth associated with loneliness. It is a Big Lie. The truth is that if your date cares about you, he or she won't pressure you to do something against God's wishes. Love puts the other person first. Jesus had a strong warning for those of us who might pressure another into sin with a Big Lie:

> Temptation to do wrong is inevitable, but woe to the man who does the tempting. So if your hand or foot causes you to sin, cut it off and throw it away. Better to enter heaven crippled than to be in hell with both of your hands and feet (Matt. 18:7, 8, TLB).

If a person claims to be a friend and then pressures you to go to bed, he or she really isn't a friend. Find someone else to go out with.

(3) *"But I can't just turn off my sexual feelings. They must be satisfied."* This is really a cop-out. Healthy men and women can live fulfilled lives without intercourse. We may *think* we can't live without sex, but that simply is not true. In fact, "surrender to all our desires obviously leads to impotence, disease, jealousies, lies, concealment, and everything that is the reverse of health, good humor, and frankness," advises C. S. Lewis. And he adds that "for any happiness, even in this world, quite a lot of restraint is going to be necessary; so the claim made by every desire, when it is strong, to be healthy and reasonable, counts for nothing."[9]

Gabrielle Brown, author of *The New Celibacy,* asserts that it is quite possible to abstain from sex and experience a new quality of life. She explains:

> People may then find that they are able to begin to experience a quality of attention that makes them more tuned in to feelings of intimacy, tenderness and fulness of love in the relationship, as well as in other parts of their lives. Instead of being dominated by just one kind of human response—the sexual—they are free to experience other responses.[10]

(5) *"I need to reaffirm my manhood/womanhood."* Our uniqueness and strength as men and women comes from our relationship with Christ, not from how sexually desirable we are to others. Affirming our masculinity and femininity has little to do with the sex act itself. It has lots to do with our self-concepts and how well we relate to other people on all levels of our lives. If we need to affirm our femininity or masculinity through physical attention, it's time to assess our ability to relate effectively to the opposite sex.

(6) *"I'm afraid I'll forget how."* Sex is a basic innate function of mankind. It is impossible to "forget how." Besides, practice is not what makes for a perfect sexual union. It is the expression of love and giving which gives the real beauty to the ecstacy we experience in intercourse. Two people who love each other learn together how to "do it." In addition, as Gabrielle Brown notes,

> Biologically we don't lose the ability to be sexual by not being sexual. And unless one is in a very weakened physical condition, one has the potential to be sexual all one's life. Yet the deceptive

impression has been created that one must be sexually active to remain healthy.[11]

(7) *"But I need some experience before I get married."* Not true. As we just noted, one of the joys of marriage is learning to respond to each other sexually, to discover this great act of intimacy. And a study of women conducted by the American Institute of Family Relations recently found that neither the delay of marriage or a lack of previous sexual experience was a hindrance to good sexual adjustment in marriage.[12]

Men have been taught to get some experience before marriage because it is the culturally acceptable thing for the male to "sow a few wild oats" before marriage. There is also the myth that the man must gain some experience so he can teach his virginal bride. These ideas are counter to biblical teaching. Men should be thinking of women as equals under Christ—as friends, not as sex objects created solely for physical enjoyment.

(8) *"How will I know that we will be sexually compatible after marriage unless we find out beforehand?"* This is another concern that arises out of our preoccupation with sexual performance. Many people fear they will get stuck with a sexual "dud" unless they have intercourse before marriage and find out what kind of lover that person is. But there is another major point to consider: people change. "Duds" can improve and "great lovers" can encounter problems that render them "duds." In marriage two people commit themselves to working out problems, and they attain sexual compatibility by sharing what gives them pleasure. Studies indicate that premarital experience isn't a dependable barometer of what marital sex will be like. The act of love-making is an aspect of marriage, in which prayer, trust in God, and commitment to one's partner must all work together. If you seek God's guidance and his assurance that the person you want to marry is the right choice for you, and if you are committed to working with that person to attain sexual compatibility, then you can be assured that "all things will work together for good" (Rom. 8:28).

(9) *"But we're planning to get married. Doesn't that make a difference?"* The answer is "no." So were lots of other couples who had sexual relations along with plans for marriage and then broke up. Leonard Benson recently conducted a study of

seventy-five students over thirty years of age. He found a total of 653 romances, an average of 8.7 per person in a lifetime. "In over a third, the most intense romances did not lead to marriage," he noted.[13] *Seventeen* magazine claims:

> Twice as many engagements are broken among couples who had intercourse.... Furthermore ... these couples are more likely to be divorced or separated or to indulge in adultery. One way or another, premarital intimacy is more closely connected to broken relationships than to solid ties.[13]

(10) *"Since the laws about fornication were written before birth control, doesn't our new technology change everything?"* New technology never has and never will change God's laws. They are absolute, timeless, and just. God's plan for intercourse was and still is to unite man and woman as "one flesh" (Gen. 2:24). Harry N. Hollis, Jr. offers further insight:

> The bridal theology of the Bible is significant in understanding sex, for it gives us a pattern for a covenant relation between people. The metaphor of marriage between God and his people demonstrates the possibility and the significance of such a covenant between a man and woman (Isa. 62:4-5).[14]

The significance of the marriage covenant and the marriage bed has not changed in God's view because of the technology of birth control.

(11) *"If intercourse is forbidden, is it OK to go* almost *that far?"* Or, in the words of a date of a friend of ours, "If we can't have intercourse, can't we have oral sex? That's not fornication, is it?" People wonder just how close to the edge of sin they can walk and still squeak by.

Oral sex, mutual masturbation, and what our parents used to call "heavy petting" is out of the question. Walking close to temptation—and looking for subtle ways to "get around" God's law while remaining technically within it—is not a true Christian walk. A sexual encounter which does not result in intercourse is still a sexual sin, and falls short of the expectations of the Master.

Those are pretty sobering statements in response to the arguments for premarital sex. In view of them and with the Bi ble's commandments, for the single Christian there obviously is no alternative to abstinence before marriage.

But What If It's Too Late?

We recognize that few people who read these words will be virgins. Almost all of us have fallen short of God's mark for sexual abstinence before marriage. Of course, many of you have already been married and have had to suffer through an abrupt end to sexual intimacy as your marriage dissolved. Many of you have had sexual relations since marriage. Maybe you're involved in a sexual relationship right now, or you're looking for a sexual partner. You may be wondering at this point how you could ever change your lifestyle. Well, if so, we have good news for you.

God loves us. He desires to make us whole people—free from the bondage of sin. He desires that we confess our sins—sexual sins included—and receive forgiveness. Jesus said, "Everyone who commits sin is a slave to sin" (John 8:34). But when we ask Jesus for forgiveness, he has promised us freedom from this bondage (John 8:36). Hollis notes:

> When we accept God's forgiveness, we are in a position to deal with specific sexual sins. These sins often create anxiety which can cause us to seek relief in further acts of sexual exploitation. Forgiveness can cleanse us of the guilt and anxiety that lurk within us when we commit sexual transgressions.[15]

As we noted earlier, much guilt can result from falling short of God's desires for our lives. But we don't need to keep carrying around a load of guilt and despair. Evans counsels, "Guilt is intended to lead us to confession and repentance. Once it has accomplished that purpose, it should end. Continuing to feel guilty may be an evidence that you do not believe that God is faithful and just in forgiving and cleansing you. Believe that God *has* forgiven and forgotten your sin."[16]

When you have done this, ask God for the strength to further resist sexual temptation. Ask him to make you wise and strong enough to say "no" when opportunities arise—no matter how much you desire sexual intimacy at that moment. And continue to study the Word, for it is the only way to know Jesus and the ultimate truth. The results will be an "unknown FREEDOM—a freedom from fear, from worry, a freedom from wrong habits, a freedom to love, a freedom to express the full personality as God meant this to be expressed when He created you as an individual."[17]

And if you fail again in the future, don't despair. God will not reject you. "Ask forgiveness, pick yourself up, and try again," encourages C. S. Lewis. And he wisely adds:

> Very often what God first helps us towards is not the virtue itself but just this power of always trying again. For however important chastity (or courage, or truthfulness, or any other virtue) may be, this process trains us in habits of the soul while are more important still. It cures our illusions about ourselves and teaches us to depend on God. We learn, on the one hand, that we cannot trust ourselves even in our best moments, and, on the other, that we need not despair even in our worst, for our failures are forgiven. The only fatal thing is to sit down content with anything less than perfection.[18]

Avoiding Sexual Sin

There are several additional things you can do to lessen the temptation of sexual sin:

(1) *Don't be caught in places where temptations can run wild.* If you are tempted towards sex, or you feel your date has physical affection on his or her mind, don't invite him or her to your place where you'll be alone and vulnerable. Avoid candlelight dinners, or any other kind of romantic evening, at home. Keep yourself from being overwhelmed by temptation.

(2) *Go on group dates.* It is difficult to be tempted when you are not alone with someone.

(3) *Let relationships develop gradually.* Be patient. Concentrate on getting to know what is inside a person, not just what is beneath their clothing. This is the more difficult route to intimacy, but it breeds a deeper love. And as years go by, a love built on this foundation will last much longer than one which rushes into sex. Often when a dating couple gets involved in a sexual relationship one will get bored, and the other will end up feeling rejected, bitter, and used.

(4) *Go out on active dates.* Try planning dates around sports activities such as tennis, racquetball, or roller-skating. Expend your energies in a constructive way.

(5) *Set some standards for yourself before you go out.* Talk about these standards with your date. Agree upon just how much display of affection you feel comfortable with. You don't venture beyond the limits you set. Make sure that your display of affection is in balance, and consistent, with the amount of actual affection you feel toward each other. Remember that it is important to talk about standards *before* you get into a "hot and heavy" situation with your date. Each of you need to discuss just how "far" you can go without inciting lust or a temptation that can't be resisted.

(6) *Say "no" and mean it.* Many men have been taught that when a woman says "no" she often means "maybe." With some persistence, men are taught, they can reach their goal of having sex with the woman. Women, say "no" strongly and firmly. And men, times are changing; you may need to say "no" at times, too, and stick with that decision.

We will be the first to admit that living God's standards for the expression of human sexuality is not always easy. But it is truly "the more excellent way." And it is the *only* way to a complete relationship with Jesus.

Cherie's Comment

It seems to me that the sexual issue is one of the main reasons many single people don't experience the fullness of a relationship with Jesus. I keep wanting to say, "Come on, try abstinence. What have you got to lose?" Just give Jesus a chance to show you what he can do in your life when you surrender everything—every desire—to him."

So many people are like the monkey I once saw in a cartoon who was a captive of a narrow-mouthed glass jar, simply because he wouldn't let go of the marbles inside. I was like that monkey for a long, long time. Now I long for single people to know the pure joy of living a life of surrender to Jesus.

Intimacy and love encompass so much more than just the physical union of two bodies. And that is why God has asked us to keep physical union within the ideal context of intimate love—the lifetime commitment of marriage.

Some of you, we suspect, are thinking right now about making such a lifetime commitment to someone. If you are, we have some thoughts on how you can know whether you are really "in marriage love."

17.

Are You in "Marriage Love"?

You're "in love" and wondering if this is the love that will result in marriage.

In essence this entire book has been about love between men and women. We've emphasized a giving love—a love that puts others first, a love that is kind and thoughtful.

Marriage love is a blend of physical love and emotional/ spiritual love. The physical love, denoted by the Greek word *eros,* is a need love. In *Sex for Christians,* Lewis B. Smedes notes:

> *Eros* is born of need. We love sexually because we need to be completed by another person. The need is far more than a need for physical release; it is a need for intimate union with the whole self of another in order to complete ourselves.[1]

The counterpart of need love is giving love. This kind of love is embodied in the Greek word *agape. Agape* love is love in action. It is a love of the will. It is the type of love Jesus exhibited when he allowed himself to be crucified for our sins. Smedes says of this love:

> *Agape* is born not of need but of fullness; it is not a seeking but a giving love; it reaches out from strength to weakness. It does not reach out for fulfillment, but to fill emptiness. It does not yearn to get what it needs, but empties itself to give what the other needs.[2]

Agape love says, "I love you even though I don't like you at this very moment." It is the type of love Paul speaks of in 1 Corinthians 13—a love that:

—is very patient and kind,
—is never jealous or envious,
—is never boastful or proud,
—is never haughty or selfish or rude,
—does not demand its own way,
—is not irritable or touchy,
—does not hold grudges,
—is never glad about injustice, but rejoices when truth wins,
—is loyal no matter the cost,
—always believes in others and wants what is best for them.

Agape is the ideal. While we strive towards it, only God—who is perfect—truly attains it. If we wait to achieve perfect *agape* before marrying, we will wait forever. All marriages are made up of selfish, sinful people. The beauty of love is that God's grace allows us to grow in an *agape* relationship, to share together in creating a good marriage. The best marriages also contain that spark of *eros,* which grows and matures throughout the relationship. *Agape* is wonderful, but as the Lord points out, we are to have *agape* for all people. And we certainly don't want to marry just anyone!

It is when *eros* takes control of a relationship that we can get sidetracked. This is the feeling that is often called infatuation. Ray E. Short, author or *Sex, Love or Infatuation: How Can I Really Know?,* notes, "Infatuation is pseudo-love or false love. It is romantic quicksand. And woe be unto you if you mistake it for real love, then go on to act as if it actually were."[3]

Infatuation is a selfish love built on *eros* alone. It demands that its needs be met. It responds only to emotional stimuli. It is best thought of as an adult version of the childhood crush. The best test of whether you are involved in a relationship built on infatuation is the test of time. We know people who were first attracted to each other with feelings we'd call infatuation. But as they grew to know each other, those feelings gradually changed into a deep love. True love survives through time. A relationship that remains on the infatuation level will not.

In his book on love and infatuation, Ray Short presents a

number of insightful questions that can help a single person know if his or her love is the kind successful marriages are built on. We've taken some of those questions and molded them into an eleven-point test.[4] If you think you may be in love, honestly ask yourself the following questions:

(1) *What is your major attraction to each other?* In infatuation, the major attraction is almost always physical, or based on an isolated characteristic such as an outgoing personality. It is selfish and materialistic in that it is based on externals: we respond to a pretty face, or a nice body, or a good conversationlist, or a fun person to be with . . . and decide that being with him or her is "love."

In true love, however, we are attracted to a person's total personality. Their inner qualities are as appealing to us as their physical appearance. It takes time to get to know a person's inner beauty. That is why time is the great killer of infatuation. A true love relationship takes time to build, because it takes time to truly get to know and love another person.

(2) *How many factors attracted you to each other?* Obviously, the more factors that attract and hold two people, the greater the possibility they will weather storms of discontent. In infatuation, the factors holding people together are few—usually sexual. But people can be infatuated for other reasons—such as sharing an enthusiasm for athletics, an interest in the opera, or an involvement in a political cause.

In a true love relationship many factors attract. We share several viewpoints and activities in common. We know how the other acts and reacts to a number of situations. If your current relationship were to result in marriage, could you men be "thoughtful of her needs and honor her?" Could you be partners in receiving God's blessings (1 Pet. 3:7)? Women, could you submit to your husband as to the Lord (Eph. 5:22)? Men, could you love your mate unselfishly, as Christ loved his church and died for her (Eph. 5:25)?

How will you know whether you can truly submit and protect? You'll know if you've taken the time to get to know each other well. To know each other means you will be attracted in many ways.

(3) *How did your relationship begin?* In infatuation, a rela-

tionship will begin quickly. We are attracted by a few things and off we go into "love."

True love only develops with time. There is no such thing as love at first sight—only infatuation at first sight (although it is certainly possible for infatuation to gradually develop into love). True love relationships start slowly and evenly. In biblical times a betrothal lasted a year. A couple became engaged and then waited. During this year of engagement, they got to know each other. That certainly taught patience. Short says,

> Time must be allowed for a lasting love relationship to develop. Real love will awaken at the *right* time—will bud and blossom and bloom in all its fullness as a man and woman grow together and learn to know each other, thereby reaching the point of deciding to make a total commitment to one another for life. One doesn't fall in and out of this kind of love.[5]

(4) *How does romance affect your personality?* Do you daydream all day long? Do you neglect work or studies? If so, you're probably infatuated. Love should have an organizing effect on you. Your motivation level should increase. There's a bright new spot in your life, and the joy of that relationship should propel you to greater heights, both in actions and thoughts. But it shouldn't cause you to lose interest in the more mundane things of each day. It should also cause you to attack daily routine jobs with renewed vigor. Love brings growth.

(5) *How do you view the other person?* If you're infatuated, the person you're dating is the "only person in the world." You "only have eyes for him." You'll neglect family and friends. Being with your one-and-only takes priority over all other responsibilities.

Kenny's Comments:
I have this tendency to get intense in my dating relationships. It arose, I think, from a sense of insecurity and panic about getting older and still not being married. I spent a lot of time with one woman I was dating—too much time, as it turns out. Without the interchange with our friends, our relationship turned inward and began stagnating. I started relying too heavily on her for all my emotional support. The more inward and

isolated our relationship became, the more demanding I got and the more we stagnated. We also saw less of our family and friends.

Actually, I can think of two relationships during which this happened. Each time, when the relationship ended, I had to sheepishly call friends and say, "Let's get together again." And I had to endure their universal retort, "Where have you been?"

(6) *How do others view you?* One of the best indicators of the "rightness" of a relationship is how parents and close friends view it. In recalling the two relationships that turned inward and died, Kenny also recalls that both of those relationships were not viewed favorably by his friends and family members. Often those who are closest to us know better than we do if a relationship is built on love or infatuation. Consider their counsel. It is often valid.

It's important to remember that the person you are dating could become your husband or wife. If so, you'll be sharing him or her all the time with your family and friends. Smoothly flowing relationships with our loved ones make our marriages flow much better too. Those of you who have already been married know this fact all too well! But we'd be willing to bet that some of you disregarded the advice of parents and friends when you got married. Letha Scanzoni notes:

> Most studies of divorce show that people who eventually dissolve their marriages are, among other things, likely to be those who rejected the advice of parents and/or friends not to marry a certain person.[6]

(7) *What does separation do for the romance?* If you're infatuated, separation cools romance, because it is based on such a superficial foundation. If you're in real love, though, "absence makes the heart grow fonder." Gian Carlo Menotti once said, "I know of no better definition of love than the one given by Proust—'love is space and time measured by the heart.'" True love survives separation because the relationship is built on factors of personality and spiritual and mental closeness. There is a sense in which people in love commune with each

other, even though apart. That, too, helps the relationship grow in absence.

(8) *How do quarrels affect your relationship?* A couple who are infatuated experience peaks and valleys of emotions. Quarrels may be frequent and severe. Fights start over minor things. Watching such a couple quarrel, one sometimes can't help but make comparisons with little children fighting over marbles, baseballs, or whose "daddy" is bigger or smarter.

A couple in love, however, are not easily provoked. They are longsuffering and forgiving. "Many waters cannot quench love, neither can floods drown it," we read in Song of Solomon (8:7, TLB). Of course, even people who have been happily married for decades will have fights. No relationship, no set of two people, is perfect. But in a relationship striving towards the ideal of *agape,* conflict is managed and used constructively. Couples work to communicate. They air grievances and work to find understanding. As a result, they grow closer to each other and to God.

(9) *How do you refer to your relationship?* This may seem like a simple tip, but it is a good test. Do you refer to your relationship with the word "we"? If so, that's an indication you may be truly in love. If your conversation is sprinkled with references to "me," "I," and "mine," you're revealing your own selfishness and the likelihood that the relationship is built on selfishness, hence infatuation. Love's ultimate ideal, especially in marriage, is to become intimate with another, to share problems, joys, and goals. This implies a merging of self with others—a "we-ness."

Let us caution, however, that there must be a balance of "we-ness." A constant emphasis on "we" can be an unhealthy sign—an indication of excessive dependence on one another rather than on God. Each of us has a separate identity. If, in stressing "we-ness," we stifle our individual growth, the relationship will stagnate. It is good to be a "we," but not just a "we."

(10) *What is your attitude towards each other?* Jealousy and selfishness are interrelated. But if either is present, a relationship is probably built on infatuation. When we're infatuated, we're concerned with having our own needs met. We become possessive and unbending. We are likely to be unforgiving. If

you'll recall the power of *eros* as a need love, you'll see that this fits with the traits we've just listed.

In true love, on the other hand, the ideal is to meet the needs of the one we love. His or her desires should come first in our thinking. True, we're all selfish and petty at times; we do experience jealousy. But in a love relationship, we should be constantly working towards the goal of putting our partner's needs before our own.

(11) *How do you relate to each other spiritually?* Is Jesus Christ the center of your relationship? Do you pray and study God's word together? Do you worship him together? A relationship built on God's love involves three people—you, the other person, and God. If he is not welcome in your relationship, it can more easily become a relationship built only on *eros* and selfish sexual expressions. If you're afraid to bring the Lord into your relationship because you'll be convicted of guilt, then most likely you are infatuated.

Now, after all these comments on the practical and spiritual aspects of love, we want to say that there is definitely a place in love relationships for the spark of romance. Love needs that elusive quality we sometimes refer to as "chemistry." The feelings of excitement—like the heart beating a little faster at the sound of a loved one's voice, the desire to give him or her special gifts, or the pleasure of just gazing into his or her eyes—are all important in true love. These are the special sparks we all hope will continue through the seasons of married love. But without a firm commitment and a striving toward *agape* love, they are not strong enough to support a long-term relationship.

We hope all these tips help you sort through the nature of any relationships you're currently involved with. They may also help you sort through past relationships, to see areas of your strengths and weaknesses. We hope the tips will also help you when you get involved in future relationships. Being in love, God's way, is a wonderful experience. Don't sell yourself short by falling for infatuation. Hold out for God's best—real love. As Short says:

> *Real love* exists when your strong tender feelings for each other are balanced by reason and deep respect. You care just as much

for the other person's welfare and fulfillment as you do for your own. Judgments about the person are quite objective and rational. The two of you share many values and ideas in common. You share similar goals and ideals. In short, you are matched as well as mated.[7]

If you've passed this 'love test' and feel you are ready to consider marriage, we have one other word of advice—see a Christian marriage and family counselor. Premarital counseling is of utmost importance. In counseling you will be given the chance to better understand yourself and your potential mate. You will receive communication tips. You will have a chance to explore—before marriage—any potentially damaging traits or characteristics you possess. Then, under guidance of the counselor, the two of you can begin to work towards understanding these potential pitfalls in your future marriage.

Oh yes, if you desire to marry, enjoy your life together. We rejoice with you, for there are few things on earth more precious than the love of a man and a woman.

The Final Conversation

In the end, was the final conversation . . . (this one at a Mexican restaurant after ten straight hours of typing the final manuscript. Although her head was swimming and her eyes were bloodshot, Cherie still was awake enough to pull up Kenny's head before it plopped into the *salsa* as he fell asleep in mid-sentence):

"Done."

"Kenny, I feel like I've given birth. Writing this book has been an experience."

"Giving birth only takes nine months, Cherie. It took two years to get this baby down on paper."

"Yes, much has happened. I feel considerably older and wiser."

"Older, yes. Wiser?"

"You know, when I think about it, I've really grown in my understanding of relationships these two years."

"I have, too, Cherie. It seems like every time I began studying a topic—like confrontation, or parental influences, or how to ask someone out—God provided an experience so I had to practice what I was preaching."

"That happened to me, too. I hope we've been honest in sharing our experiences and the message God gave us to share."

"I feel like we have, Cherie. But you know, I didn't realize dating encompassed so many subjects. Writing about it is a bit overwhelming. I think we only scratched the surface of what could be said."

"Yeah, the issue's a big one. And complicated. But the bottom line is, 'Will this book change lives?'"

"Well, Cherie, it has changed ours. And if others feel we've been honest and truth-seeking, then it will change their lives too."

"I know there was lots of interest in our project. 'Hurry up and finish,' people said to me, when I told them what we were doing. 'I need to read that.'"

"No doubt about it. All singles are concerned with dating. I hope our message of victory and hope comes through loud and clear. Let's face it: if we grew, others can grow, too."

"That's true, Kenny. What a neat thought. I'm glad we wrote this book. I'm glad the Lord allowed us to give birth to it."

"Me, too."

(And thus ended the writing of *Dating and Relating: A Guide for Single Christians,* with Cherie and Kenny both thinking: "Thanks, Lord.")

Notes

Chapter 1

1. Bert H. Hodges, "Any Body Can Be Spiritual," *His,* May 1981, p. 18.
2. A. Wetherall Johnson, "Genesis—Lesson 19," (San Antonio, Tex.: Bible Study Fellowship, 1960), p. 5.

Chapter 2

1. Raymond C. Ortlund, *Lord, Make My Life a Miracle* (Glendale, Calif.: Regal Books, 1974), p. 31.
2. Anthony Ash, "Don't Quit," *Single Again Newsletter,* February 1977, p. 4.

Chapter 3

1. Marie Edwards and Eleanor Hoover, *The Challenge of Being Single* (Los Angeles: J. P. Tarcher, 1974), pp. 23-24.
2. Ibid., p. 26.
3. John Fischer, "A Single Person's Identity," Discovery Papers (mimeographed paper distributed by Discovery Publishing, Palo Alto, California, 1973).
4. Mark W. Lee, "The Church and the Unmarried," *It's O.K. to Be Single,* ed. Gary R. Collins (Waco, Tex.: Word Books, 1976), p. 49.
5. Fischer, "Single Person's Identity."
6. "A Conversation with Ann Kiemel," *Solo,* September/October 1979, pp. 8-13.

Chapter 4

1. Maggie Scarf, "The Promiscuous Woman," *Psychology Today,* July 1980, p. 87.
2. W. Hugh Missildine, *Your Inner Child of the Past* (New York: Simon & Schuster, 1963), p. 31.
3. Information for this section taken from pp. 85-315 of Missildine, *Your Inner Child.* Used by permission of the publisher.
4. Catherine Marshall, *Something More* (New York: Avon Books, 1976), p. 54.
5. Ibid., p. 55.
6. Ibid., p. 59.
7. Ruth Carter Stapleton, *The Gift of Inner Healing* (Waco, Tex.: Word Books, 1977), p. x.
8. Marshall, *Something More,* p. 59.
9. Ibid.

Chapter 5
1. C. H. Spurgeon, *12 Sermons on Various Subjects* (Grand Rapids, Mich.: Baker Book House, 1974), p. 41.
2. Jo Ludin, *The Hoax of Romance* (Englewood Cliffs, N.J.: Prentice-Hall, 1981), p. VIII.
3. Ibid., pp. 93-97.
4. Lewis B. Smedes, *Sex for Christians* (Grand Rapids, Mich.: Wm. B. Eerdmans Publishing Co., 1976), p. 50.
5. Ludin, *The Hoax of Romance,* p. 95.

Chapter 6
1. Dave Coffman and Lee Nicoloff, "Running Group Therapy" (Paper presented at the University of Texas, 1980).
2. Diane Blacker, *Harmony: How to Let God's Gifts Come Together in Your Life* (Old Tappan, N.J.: Fleming H. Revell Co., 1978), p. 120.
3. Gini Andrews, *Your Half of the Apple* (Grand Rapids, Mich.: Zondervan Publishing House, 1972), p. 101.
4. Blacker, *Harmony,* p. 120.
5. Ibid.
6. Ibid.
7. Donna Axum, *The Outer You ... The Inner You* (Waco, Tex.: Word Books, 1978), p. 36.
8. "Today's Living" (bulletin printed by Syndicate Magazines, New York, for distribution by health food stores).

Chapter 7
1. Joyce Brothers, *How to Get What You Want Out of Life* (New York: Ballantine Books, 1978), p. 227.
2. Much of the inspiration for this section comes from Audrey Gellis, *How to Meet Men* (New York: Popular Library, 1978).
3. Marie Edwards and Eleanor Hoover, *The Challenge of Being Single* (Los Angeles: J. P. Tarcher, 1974), p. 162.

Chapter 8
1. Quoted in Elaine Walster and G. William Walster, *A New Look at Love* (Reading, Mass.: Addison-Wesley Publishing Co., 1978), p. 31.

Chapter 11
1. David H. Roper, "Jonathan and David" Discovery Papers (mimeographed paper distributed by Discovery Publishing, Palo Alto, California, 1973).

Chapter 13
1. J. Grant Howard, *The Trauma of Transparency* (Portland, Ore.: Multnomah Press, 1979), p. 198.
2. Alan Loy McGinnis, *The Friendship Factor: How to Get Closer to the People You Care For* (Minneapolis, Minn.: Augsburg Publishing House, 1979), p. 39.
3. Ron Adler and Neil Towne, *Looking Out/Looking In* (San Francisco: Holt, Rinehart & Winston, 1975), p. 69.
4. McGinnis, *The Friendship Factor*, p. 35.
5. Ibid., p. 122.
6. Ibid., p. 97.
7. Ibid.

Chapter 14
1. Muriel James and Louis Savaray, *The Heart of Friendship* (San Francisco: Harper and Row Pubs., 1978), p. 166.
2. Ibid., p. 171.
3. Mark Knapp, *Social Intercourse* (Boston: Allyn and Bacon, 1978), p. 164.
4. Carole Altman, "Women! It's Up to You to Make Your Relationships Work," *Forum*, January 1980, p. 17.
5. David Augsburger, *Caring Enough to Confront* (Glendale, Calif.: Regal Books, 1979), p. 111.
6. Ibid., p. 64.

Chapter 15
1. Toby Hempel, *How to Get Over a Broken Romance* (Rouses Point, N.Y.: Globe Communications, 1980), p. 11.
2. Quoted from Calvary Chapel bulletin, Costa Mesa, Calif., 24 May 1981.
3. Patricia Chavez and Clif Cartland, *Picking Up the Pieces* (Nashville, Tenn.: Thomas Nelson, 1979), p. 131.
4. Ibid., p. 184.
5. Zev Wanderer and Tracy Cabot, *Letting Go: A Twelve-Week Personal Action Program to Overcome a Broken Heart* (New York: G. P. Putnam's Sons, 1978), p. 62.
6. Hempel, *How to Get Over a Broken Romance*, p. 20.
7. Ibid., p. 19.
8. Anonymous quote from *Single Sation News*, Santa Ana, Calif., February 1979.

Chapter 16
1. Jerry Evans, "Sex Before Marriage—Why Should We Wait?" *His,* May 1981, p. 1.

2. Lewis B. Smedes, *Sex for Christians* (Grand Rapids, Mich.: Wm. B. Eerdmans Publishing Co., 1976), p. 30.

3. Bert H. Hodges, "Any Body Can Be Spiritual," *His,* May 1981, p. 17.

4. Smedes, *Sex for Christians,* p. 134.

5. Evans, "Sex Before Marriage," p. 4.

6. Ibid.

7. Harold Ivan Smith, "Sex and Singleness the Second Time Around," *Christianity Today,* 25 May 1979, p. 1.

8. Smedes, *Sex for Christian,* p. 104.

9. C. S. Lewis, *Mere Christianity* (New York: Macmillan Publishing Co., 1943), p. 93.

10. Gabrielle Brown, *The New Celibacy* (New York: McGraw-Hill Book Co., 1980), p. 29.

11. Ibid., p. 8.

12. Rusty Wright and Linda Raney Wright, *Dynamic Sex* (San Bernadino, Calif.: Here's Life Pubs., 1979), p. 45.

13. Quoted in David A. Seamands, "Sex: Inside and Outside Marriage," *The Secrets of Our Sexuality,* ed. Gary Collins (Waco, Tex.: Word Books, 1976), p. 160.

14. Harry N. Hollis, Jr., "A Christian Model for Sexual Understanding and Behavior," in *The Secrets of Our Sexuality,* ed. Gary R. Collins (Waco, Tex.: Word Books, 1976), p. 79.

15. Ibid., p. 78.

16. Evans, "Sex Before Marriage," p. 7.

17. A. Wetherall Johnson, "John—Lesson 13" (San Antonio, Tex.· Bible Study Fellowship, 1960), p. 5.

18. Lewis, *Mere Christianity,* p. 94.

Chapter 17

1. Lewis B. Smedes, *Sex for Christians* (Grand Rapids, Mich.: Wm. B. Eerdmans Publishing Co., 1976), p. 92.

2. Ibid., p. 93.

3. Ray E. Short, *Sex, Love, or Infatuation: How Can I Really Know?* (Minneapolis, Minn.: Augsburg Publishing House, 1978), p. 16.

4. These ideas are taken, by permission, from pp. 52-155 of Short, *Sex, Love or Infatuation.*

5. Short, *Sex, Love or Infatuation,* p. 16.

6. Letha Scanzoni, *Why Wait? A Christian View of Premarital Sex* (Grand Rapids, Mich.: Baker Book House, 1975), p. 87.

7. Short, *Sex, Love or Infatuation,* p. 17.